MORE PRAISE FOR RAISING THE BAR

"My son Gary's awesome true Clif Bar story, as told in this book, brings tears to my eyes, sends chills up my spine, and gives joy to my heart."

—CLIFFORD ERICKSON

"I can relate to a guy who's faced a few challenges on a bike. Reading about Gary's adventures in the mountains, on his bike, and with Clif Bar inspires me. Gary understands the meaning of adventure in life and business."

—TYLER HAMILTON, PROFESSIONAL CYCLIST

"Whether I've been climbing or just visiting with Gary, he motivates me to consider what's possible. He has a powerful dreaming mind and a kind of vision to make our world a better place. It's awesome to see Gary and the people at Clif Bar turn their business into a way of life."

—RON KAUK, CLIMBER

"Gary Erickson is one of my heroes. His book is a story about bridging personal interests with business, about thinking big in a time when the world is encouraging us to think small."

—JULIA BUTTERFLY HILL, ACTIVIST AND AUTHOR,

CONSCIOUS CHOICE MAGAZINE

"If you're disgruntled with the corruption within corporate America, you will applaud this autobiography. *Raising the Bar* is an inspiring story which shows that in life, sometimes the guarantee of instant financial wealth is the path not chosen. Highly recommended."

—*CHICAGO ATHLETE* MAGAZINE

"Beware. After reading this book, you may just find yourself on a long, lone bike ride, dreaming up some new company or idea or mentally arranging your resume so you can send it to Clif Bar's human resources department."

—*VELO NEWS*

"What makes Erickson's book worth reading is that he's as honest about his mistakes as his successes."

—*NEWSWEEK*

"*Raising the Bar* is great inspiration for any entrepreneur committed to maintaining principles while raising profits."

—DAILY COURT REVIEW

"Erickson tells the fascinating story of his life. More important, he shares his beliefs about following your passion, having the freedom to create, sustaining a business, and living responsibly."

—DES MOINES BUSINESS RECORD

"Inspirational. Gary Erickson shows us that the many attributes that make us successful in life also make us successful in business."

—HARVARD BUSINESS SCHOOL WORKING KNOWLEDGE

"What makes the book fresh is Erickson's honesty and humility."

—BUSINESSWEEK

RAISING THE BAR

RAISING
THE BAR

INTEGRITY AND PASSION
IN LIFE AND BUSINESS

A JOURNEY TOWARD SUSTAINING
YOUR BUSINESS, BRAND, PEOPLE,
COMMUNITY, AND THE PLANET

GARY ERICKSON WITH LOIS LORENTZEN

JOSSEY-BASS
A Wiley Imprint
www.josseybass.com

Published by Jossey-Bass
A Wiley Imprint
989 Market Street, San Francisco, CA 94103-1741
www.josseybass.com

Text design by Leif Eric Arneson.

Jossey-Bass books and products are available through most bookstores. To contact Jossey-Bass directly call our Customer Care Department within the U.S. at 800-956-7739, outside the U.S. at 317-572-3986, or fax 317-572-4002.

Jossey-Bass also publishes its books in a variety of electronic formats. Some content that appears in print may not be available in electronic books.

Library of Congress Cataloging-in-Publication Data

Erickson, Gary.
   Raising the bar : integrity and passion in life and business, the story
of Clif Bar, Inc. / Gary Erickson with Lois Lorentzen.—1st ed.
      p.   cm.
   Includes bibliographical references and index.
   ISBN-10 0-7879-7365-3 (alk. paper)
   ISBN-13 978-0-7879-8671-1 (paperback)
   ISBN-10 0-7879-8671-2 (paperback)
   1. Clif Bar Inc.   2. Snack food industry—United States.
I. Lorentzen, Lois Ann, 1952–   II. Title.

HD9219.U64C583   2004
338.7'6646—dc22   2004006422

Printed in the United States of America on acid-free, elementally chlorine-free, recycled paper, 30% postconsumer waste

FIRST EDITION

HB Printing 10 9 8 7 6 5 4 3 2 1
PB Printing 10 9 8 7 6 5 4 3 2 1

CONTENTS

Following the publication of *Raising the Bar,* I traveled the country giving numerous lectures and readings. Everywhere I went, people identified with my story, including entrepreneurs, cyclists, mountain climbers, and musicians. Countless individuals sent me letters about their own white-road journeys. I felt honored that people were moved by my tale; some were even inspired to take paths that went against conventional wisdom. They told me, "I was going to work for a corporation, but now I'm going to move West and become an artist," or "I am not going to sell my company because I read your book," or "I too hope to ride in the Alps and take the white roads." They chose the entrepreneurial path, uncomfortable at times but always exciting.

As I witnessed the response to *Raising the Bar,* I felt grateful, grateful to our past and present employees, distributors, brokers, retailers, consultants, vendors, manufacturers, and to all the consumers who believe in our product and company.

I hope you enjoy our story and are inspired to take your own *walk around the block.*

TO KIT, MY PARTNER IN LIFE AND BUSINESS.
TO MY PARENTS, CLIFF AND MARY,
FOR ALLOWING ME THE FREEDOM TO EXPLORE
WHO I AM. AND TO CLIF PEOPLE FOR
BELIEVING IN THE VISION.

RAISING THE BAR

CHAPTER I

SEND THEM HOME

(OR WHY WALK AWAY FROM $60 MILLION?)

Monday, April 17, 2000, and I was about to become a very rich man. Today my business partner and I would sell Clif Bar Inc., our company, for $120 million. I would have "more money than Carter has Pills," as my dad always said. I'd never have to work again. But instead of feeling excited, I felt nauseated constantly and hadn't slept well in weeks.

Attorneys from Clif Bar and Company X had worked feverishly all weekend. Head honchos flew in from the Midwest to finalize the details. Finally it was late Monday morning, and I stood in the office waiting to go out and sign the contract. Out of nowhere I started to shake and couldn't breathe. I'd climbed big mountains, raced bicycles, played horn in jazz concerts: I handled pressure well, so this first-ever anxiety attack took me by surprise. I told my partner that I needed to walk around the block. Outside, as I started across the parking lot, I began to weep, overwhelmed. "How did I get here? Why am I doing this?" I kept walking. Halfway around the block I stopped dead in my tracks, hit by an epiphany. I felt in my gut, "I'm not done," and then "I don't have to do this." I began to laugh, feeling free, instantly. I turned around, went back to the office and told my partner, "Send them home. I can't sell the company."

"I'm not done."

"I don't have to
do this . . ."

GARY & CLIFFORD
—STUART SCHWARTZ

Now, selling the company is a distant thought. People thought I was crazy to pass up wealth beyond my wildest dreams. Investment bankers told me the company would go under within six months. My partner thought Clif Bar couldn't compete against the big companies and demanded that I buy her out.

Today, instead of "hanging out on tropical islands" or writing big checks to my favorite causes, I'm working harder than I've worked in years. Why? This book is the story of why. It's about following your passion and gut, about the freedom to create, about getting a company's mojo back, about the jazz of business, about sustaining a business over the long haul, about living responsibly in a community and on the earth.

➤ FOLLOWING THE NATURAL PATH, OR HOW DID I GET TO THE POINT OF SELLING?

In 1990, ten years before the almost sale of Clif Bar Inc., I lived in a garage in Berkeley with my dog, skis, climbing gear, and two trumpets. One of my passions was long-distance cycling. During one day-long 175-mile ride with my buddy Jay Thomas, I came up with the idea for Clif Bar. We'd been gnawing on some "other" energy bars all day. Suddenly, I couldn't take another bite, despite being famished and needing to eat to keep going. It came to me: "I could make a better bar than this." I call that moment "the epiphany." Clif Bar exists because I wanted to make a better product for myself and for my friends. Two years later, after countless hours in Mom's kitchen, I had a recipe that worked.

Clif Bar Inc. got its official launch in 1992. We make portable, convenient, nutritious energy bars for athletes and health-minded people. Today we're one of the leaders in the category of energy and nutrition bars, and our products include Clif Bar, Luna Bar, Mojo Bar, Luna Glow, Clif Builders, and Clif Shot. Clif Bar Inc. is also the largest privately held company in its category. By the time we nearly sold the company, Clif Bar had grown from a guy making bars in his mom's kitchen to a company with $40 million in annual sales. I loved Clif Bar—the product, the people, the spirit of the company. I felt that there was more ahead for Clif Bar, yet, on April 17, 2000, I nearly sold the company. Why?

One of the main reasons I didn't fight the sale of Clif Bar Inc. was that selling seemed like the norm. The story went—and still goes—like this: You're an entrepreneur. Your company grows and begins to feel too big for you. You're tired, stressed out, and working really hard. You become convinced that you can't compete against larger companies. You also become convinced that you can sell and maintain the company's—and your own—integrity. An offer comes along. The money is appealing. You sell the company.

I had watched many peer companies go up for sale. Our archrival PowerBar went (like Clif) from humble kitchen origins to being the leading energy bar at the time. Nestlé purchased PowerBar for around $400 million, and the founder walked away with 60 percent—an outrageous amount of money. I watched my friends at Balance Bar, our other big competitor, sell to Kraft. I knew that many people began their companies

RAISING THE BAR

THE STORY OF CLIF BAR, INC.

with exit strategies in mind. I didn't, yet accepted why people would exit, just as almost everyone accepted why we would sell the company. It seemed like selling was the *natural path,* the normal culmination to starting a small but successful company.

> THE FEAR FACTOR

If I became convinced that selling was the norm, a big part of deciding to sell my own company had to do with fear. For years the refrain around Clif was "We are putting in all this work, and it could evaporate in a day," and "We need external funding to grow." We feared failure. My former partner and I told our employees that, with the sale of PowerBar to Nestlé and Balance Bar to Kraft, the two largest food companies in the world were competing against us, and we didn't want it all to disappear. It seemed to make sense. Nestlé, a company with sales of $65 billion annually, could afford to spend $50 million to promote their product against ours. To them $50 million was pocket change; to us it was more than our entire annual sales. We feared that we couldn't survive such fierce competition without a huge infusion of capital. Our investment banker, my business partner, and popular wisdom convinced me that the big companies would marginalize us. They would blow us away in advertising and marketing.

What was going on in the company didn't always inspire fear in me. We were riding an incredible wave. Clif Bar had grown from $700,000 in annual sales in 1992 to over $40 million in 1999. I was thinking, "This is unbelievable. This is like getting on the biggest wave of life and you are actually riding it and enjoying the ride." Yet others, including my partner, feared that it could all be gone tomorrow.

Fear grew at Clif Bar. Fear kept me from performing at my best, and it paralyzed others. Looking back at how fear drained Clif Bar's spirit, I remember my days as a wilderness instructor guiding young people on trips in the spectacular Sierra Nevada range of northern California. We taught kids how to climb, how to use ropes, climbing harnesses, and techniques for climbing rock faces. One of those techniques is called *belaying*. Belaying secures the climber, using ropes and anchor, so that if the person falls, they just fall a few feet. I remember teaching kids belaying from the top of a cliff. We showed them how the rope would catch them if they fell, yet there were always students that would shout to me, "I can't do it. I can't make it. I can't climb anymore." It was their fear talking, not their actual physical ability to get over an overhang or climb a hard move. Again we'd explain the worst-case scenario, how under proper belay they would only fall a foot or two. Once they overcame the fear and started to trust they usually made it. And even if they couldn't complete the climb they could say, "I gave it my all."

Recently a former student wrote to me about a climb up the Doodad that we'd done together over twenty years ago. (The Doodad is a spectacular rock outcrop that soars a thousand feet above a northern Sierra valley floor and has a particularly airy summit block.) This student reminded me about how frightened he'd been because he couldn't see me belaying him. All he could see was a thousand feet of air beneath his feet. He was forced to fully trust the rope and me. Once he trusted and managed his fear he enjoyed the climb so much that he wrote to me about it twenty years later.

The point is that fear paralyzes. Back in 2000 fear stopped me from seeing, at least for a while, that the worst-case scenario for Clif Bar was similar to falling while on belay. You fall a foot, not to your death. Yet fear was leading us to sell the company.

> PROMISES, PROMISES

Why I almost sold also has to do with the process itself—the promises made and betrayed along the way. My business partner and I stood in front of the company and made a promise: "We are going to sell the company, but we will still be here." We gave our word that we would never sell Clif Bar to anyone who wouldn't let us continue to run the company. Now I wish that I could have been a "fly on the wall of their brains," to hear inside our employees' heads. I believe that I would have heard them laughing, thinking, "How ridiculous, they will not let you run the company." Other people knew that everything would change, but I was led to believe the impossible and deluded myself. I promised that our continued management of the company was a nonnegotiable criterion.

I NEVER FORGOT THAT COMMITMENT, yet a few weeks before the sale, the company that was going to purchase us made it very clear that our tenure as managers would be short, down to months. It shocked us to discover that within three to four months Clif Bar would move to company headquarters in the Midwest. Our employees would be on the street. This announcement came just before the contract was to be signed and the money wired. Had I been listening to my gut I would have seen this coming. I now tell people who plan to sell their companies to *watch the process carefully.* It often begins with a soft sell. At first you hear, "We love you guys. We think you are the greatest company. You are fantastic. We want you to continue with the company." The sales job is full on, and they say everything you want to hear. As time goes on you commit to the process itself and start to focus on the finish line and the money. Soon you've gone so far down the road that it seems irreversible, and you begin to give up on the promises you've made.

I have seen this happen with many peers in the food industry. Afterward they often say that they felt manipulated in the process of selling and would do it differently now. You come to believe that in the end, when you see that fat check, the rest won't matter. Keeping the employees, maintaining the integrity of your products, running the company won't seem that important. The knowledge that a lot of money will be wired into your account looms larger and larger and you say, "Well, I can live

RAISING THE BAR

THE STORY OF CLIF BAR, INC.

with that." You detach. By the end of the process I was feeling, "Let's just get this done."

What did I learn from this experience? In retrospect I realized that when you sell your company you sell your vision. You will not be able to fulfill promises made to your employees, consumers, or yourself.

> ### ➤ LISTEN TO YOUR GUT

Maybe the biggest reason that I came so close to selling the company was that I wasn't listening to my gut. I prided myself on being a person who listened to my gut. I listened to my gut when I created Clif Bar. I listened to my gut when I traveled around the world. I listened to my gut when I raced bicycles. I listened to my gut while rock climbing. I listened to my gut when I married Kit. I think I got good at acting intuitively. Operating from the gut or intuition isn't about making random or illogical choices. It's about being able to bring experience, logic, passion, and creativity to bear on the unknown, and, in a split second, make sense of it. My gut was yelling at me in the years and months preceding the sale, but I didn't listen. I detached from the process. I remember thinking, "You feel sick to your stomach, and you are not sleeping because that is what anyone would be doing in this situation. You are selling the company you started, and you don't have a choice [or so I thought]. Of course you feel bad. You wonder what will happen to the employees, to the products you have created, to the company." I thought it was natural. Yet, looking back, the feeling I was having wasn't the sort of nearly sick sensation I felt before bike races or playing music in front of hundreds of people. I call that "happy nervous." I wanted to be racing. I wanted to be playing music. It made sense. My gut knew I was doing the right thing. The nervousness or anxiety felt good, it felt right. This new anxiety felt empty. But I kept saying, "This is the way it is."

As I began to tell the people closest to me about my decision to sell, a lot of people spoke to my gut, but I couldn't hear them. The hardest person to tell was Kit, my wife. I took her to a movie and told her we were selling the company. She started to cry. She knew Clif Bar had been my life for fourteen years. She saw Clif Bar as my means of self-expression in the world. Losing Clif Bar was like taking the brush away from the artist or the horn from the hand of the musician and saying, "find another way to express yourself." She wondered how I could walk away from something like that so fast.

When I told my dad about selling the company, he was surprised. As always he was supportive, but he didn't understand my decision. I tried to sell him on the idea, yet I felt sad that a

RAISING
THE BAR

THE STORY OF CLIF BAR, INC.

" I don't cry spontaneously. I am a slow burner. My teary response to Gary's telling me he was selling Clif Bar was a total gut reaction, a visceral, emotional response. Something at my core was so sad. When I married Gary I made more money than he did ($14,000). I told him that the worst that can happen is that we lose everything. We could survive. The moment Gary said 'Send them home,' it was like a weight was lifted from him. The difference was instantaneous.

The decision not to sell was about the way we are meant to live in the world. We all choose to be in the world and this was our way of being. What was going on at Clif was so strong, so good. *We weren't finished.* "

—KIT, GARY'S WIFE

large multinational food corporation would own a product named after my father.

Every bar we produce tells the story of why I named Clif Bar after my dad. My father introduced me to the love of adventure and of being independent and free. He took my brothers and me to the mountains at a young age, teaching us how to ski in the 1960s on wood boards with bear-trap bindings. My parents made little money, but we never felt like we needed more. We took long trips across the country, camping out. We lived life to the fullest and never thought about how little money we had. Although my dad was still proud of me, I could tell that the money didn't do anything for him.

I called my friend Jay to tell him I was selling. He was speechless. He couldn't understand why I would sell. Jay and I cycled one or two thousand miles in Europe every summer. I came up with the idea for Clif Bar on a bike ride with him. He knew that Clif Bar was my passion and life; something I didn't see at the moment. He listened to me as I talked about the money and pointed out how both my language and what I was talking about had changed. No longer were we enthusiastically talking about new products, exciting sponsorships, new pro racers Clif Bar could support. I heard him saying, "What are you doing?" He thought I was getting ready to sell my soul.

My brother Randy, Clif Bar's vice president of innovation, was shocked, absolutely shocked. He didn't accept it, didn't believe it, and didn't think I should do it. In the end Randy and all these people were saying to me, "This is not you. You're a risk taker. For you, it's about the vision."

CLIMB ON HIGHER
CATHEDRAL ROCK, YOSEMITE.
—CASEY SHAW

RAISING
THE
BAR

THE STORY OF CLIF BAR, INC.

My friends and family understood that the experts are often right, but that they can't predict what happens when someone really believes. They knew that the experts weren't right about Clif Bar. They knew that I wasn't being honest with myself. I wasn't hearing my heart. I wasn't doing what I needed to do to give my gut the space and time to speak. Luckily, it kicked in anyway.

> ## ➤ KNOW WHEN TO TAKE A BREAK: EVEN A WALK AROUND THE BLOCK

My gut was so powerful the day of the sale. It was as if someone had bonked me over the head saying, "Would you just take two minutes to listen to your gut here, guy, because you are *not* listening." Something intervened and forced me to take that walk. The pace leading up to the sale was brutal, and, other than one quick trip to Baja California, I had taken no breaks. I worked long hours readying the company for sale. I flew all over the country to meet with large multinational food companies. I was wined and dined. *And I wasn't riding my bike.* Some people choose meditation, yoga, or walking as the way to ground themselves, to renew, to keep creative. I ride my bike. The best ideas I've had, including Clif Bar, came to me while cycling. I listen to my gut during long hours on my bicycle. I hadn't been riding and this meant I wasn't listening.

I still look back and wonder: What if I didn't take the walk? I made the decision to send them home in a split second, and it felt completely right. It was truly a moment of following my heart.

RAISING THE BAR

THE STORY OF CLIF BAR, INC.

In any leadership position you have to find ways to get away, to create space in your head. Obsessing twenty-four hours a day about your business is easy. It can seem that getting away, thinking about nothing, won't accomplish anything. Yet the truth is that taking a break may be the most important business move you ever make.

➤ FORKS IN THE ROAD

It took a while for me to realize that this decision was a big fork in my road. My life would change dramatically no matter what I chose. One road led to the ability to retire at forty-two with wealth beyond my wildest dreams. The other road, not selling the company, ultimately led to a Day of Reckoning—with my partner, with the competition. I knew there was no easy way out and no easy decision (well, maybe taking the money was the easy way out). Looking back, I know that if I had sold Clif Bar I would have spent the rest of my life wondering, "Did I really need to do that? Could we have made it? Could I have done it without bringing in large amounts of capital from a big company or a venture capitalist?" When I finally listened, I heard a simple message: "If you don't try, you will never know success or failure." If I walked away I'd be skipping out halfway through the journey. If I was climbing the face of Half Dome in Yosemite

Valley and a helicopter offered me a way off the rock face halfway up, I wouldn't know if I could climb to the top.

And with Clif Bar, I wasn't done with the climb.

This fork in the road was dramatic, maybe the biggest fork in my life's road up to that point. I guess my decision was dramatic, too. It's radical to choose hard work and huge risk over full retirement. But I believe that the heart of being an entrepreneur is just that: being willing to work hard and to take significant risks.

➤ RISKY BUSINESS

If you look up *entrepreneur* in the dictionary, risk is at the core of every definition. The *Webster's Third New International Dictionary* defines the word as "one who assumes the risk of a business venture." The question for every entrepreneur is, how much risk are you willing to take and at what point does the risk become too much to handle?

All of us have built-in risk meters. At a certain threshold a warning buzzer sounds. The key is to know your own risk threshold. My risk threshold is relatively high, and it

developed early through my involvement in sports and music. When I got the chance to play my first jazz solo in high school, I decided not to write my solo beforehand. I just wanted to let it flow, open to the moment of improvisation. I was frightened the week before the performance: What if I started to play in front of two hundred people and nothing came out? What if it sounded terrible? With no backup plan in mind, I went for it.

Rock climbing is a sport defined by risk. Even though my parents introduced me to skiing and hiking in Yosemite, they weren't thrilled about my passion for climbing. I assured them that I was never careless and tried to show them how climbing was safer than they perceived. For more than fifteen years, I climbed every chance I got. I loved rock and ice climbs; they were incredibly fun as well as adventurous. I was never as accomplished a climber as many of my friends, but I took countless calculated risks on rock and ice. Climbing taught me about fear, about pushing myself beyond what I thought possible, about life and its meaning.

Just as climbing and jazz improvisation have their own sets of risks, so did the parking lot decision. Some people were breathless at the risk I took and told me they never could have made that decision. I terrified my business partner when I said, "I want to beat the odds." I didn't know exactly how we would beat the odds, but I believed that we could by making the right choices about how to grow the company. I knew there were risks, but they were calculated risks. One of the calculations was that I was going to run the company. Instead of retiring I was going to work hard, really hard. Another part of the calculation was figuring out the possible consequences of my decision.

**FIRST JAZZ SOLO AT
AMERICAN HIGH SCHOOL
IN FREMONT, CALIFORNIA.**
—YEARBOOK PHOTO

RAISING THE BAR

THE STORY OF CLIF BAR, INC.

First, I risked failure. My business partner, investment bankers,
and venture capitalists could all say, "I told you so." If I failed,
the company might be worth half as much as currently valued
in less than a year. Employees would be laid off. I might think,
"I should have taken the offer when I had the chance." I risked
finding out that I wasn't up to leading the company solo. My
partner and I had led the company together, or she had been
CEO. I didn't know if I could do it. And finally, I risked losing
the vision. I might end up having to sell the company or become
so leveraged that I would be forced to compromise my vision,
values, and commitments—the very things that led me to
decide not to sell in the first place.

I couldn't know the outcome, but I calculated the risk, weighing
everything, and decided that the worst case scenario felt like
being belayed, like falling a foot rather than falling to my

death. Even if I fell a foot, my integrity, my passion for what I do, and the idea of not giving up would still be intact.

➤ WHAT ABOUT THE MONEY?

Sixty million dollars is an outrageous amount of money for a guy who started a company with $1,000 of his own money. I couldn't fathom it. Just ten years before, I was thirty-three, living in a garage with no bathroom and no heat, bringing home less than $10,000 a year. Now I could be wealthier than anyone I knew. It was like winning the lottery, plus.

The weird thing is that I could never imagine past the day that I got the money. "What do I do next?" "What am I going to do with my life?" I could never visualize what it would look like. I wasn't thinking, "Oh cool, I can buy a plane. I can buy a villa in Italy, my favorite country." Kit never got excited about what we could do with all that money. We had small children at the time. Kit would end up with more money than she ever dreamed of, more time with her husband, a partner more available for the children—an easier life. Yet she hadn't wanted me to sell Clif.

The irony is that I was very happy when I lived in the garage. I was racing my bike. I was living hand-to-mouth. I was driving

Athlinks

my 1976 Datsun 510 (purchased for $375 and held together with duct tape) to Yosemite for rock climbing weekends. I was hanging out with great friends. I enjoyed my work. *Nothing was missing* (except my beloved wife and family). I didn't start Clif Bar to make money or to fill holes in my life. I started Clif Bar because I wanted to make a better energy bar for my friends and myself.

Before starting Clif Bar I jotted down a business plan in my notebook. All I wanted was enough money to do the things I already enjoyed. My goal wasn't to become a millionaire. I wanted to make a comfortable salary, create a quality product, employ great people, work on causes I believed in, and contribute to the community. It ended up having a life of its own; growing to millions of dollars in sales, but Clif Bar was never just about the money.

I told my story to Mo Siegel, the founder of Celestial Seasonings. He asked, "Can we switch places?" Mo grew Celestial Seasonings, sold it to Kraft Foods, but continued as CEO. He traveled to India in 1986 and visited Mother Teresa at one of her hospitals. Mo told Mother Teresa that he planned to leave Celestial Seasonings and volunteer his time with nonprofit organizations. Mother Teresa told him, "Mo, your calling is not

RAISING THE BAR

THE STORY OF CLIF BAR, INC.

BERKELEY GARAGE AND DATSUN 510.
—GARY ERICKSON

RAISING THE BAR

THE STORY OF CLIF BAR, INC.

to leave your company. You can do more good in the world working in your company. Grow where you are planted." Mother Teresa told him that his calling in life was to stay with his company. Mo told me the story with regret, as if he were reliving it at that moment. If he had to do it over again, he wouldn't have sold Celestial Seasonings.

I thought I was doing something good with Clif Bar. I never thought of growing the company and selling. Why was that better than owning a company, employing people, creating great products, using the power of the company for philanthropic ends, and possibly making positive changes in the world?

Business has a purpose beyond money. We look for meaning in our lives. Business has meaning too. Walking around the block forced me to ask again, "What is Clif Bar's meaning?"

➤ REDEFINING SHAREHOLDER VALUE

Do I regret getting so far in the process that I had to walk off the altar? No, I do not. Getting to that point taught me a lot about the way business is conducted now and set me on the path to defining my own values as an entrepreneur. At the moment of my split-second decision I knew I was back on track. Clif Bar had a destiny or vocation, even though I couldn't define it then. I felt called to steward Clif Bar and what it represented.

Deciding not to sell and buying out my partner meant that Kit and I became the sole shareholders in Clif Bar Inc. We had to look deeply into what kind of return we wanted and how to maximize that return. Traditionally, shareholder value is maximized by high return on investment. The stock market is the perfect example. The first (and usually only) thing a person wants from an investment in a public company is a financial return on the investment. If you buy a share for $10, you hope that by the end of the following year your share will be worth $20. If that happens, you'll probably brag to your friends about the hot stock you discovered. Yet there are questions you may not be asking. Does the company make sustainable decisions as it seeks high investment returns? Does it make decisions for the long haul? If a company is taking off, should investors ignore their own values for financial gain? To me shareholder value is long-term stewardship or sustainability.

Kit and I decided that we want a business model that can sustain itself without depending on outside capital to grow. We want to grow at a pace where we can remain profitable. We put most of the money back into the company to keep it healthy. We know we need profit, but profit is not the reason we exist. Profit enables Clif Bar to remain healthy and to do good over the long haul.

Shareholder return is knowing that we create healthy products that people want. Shareholder value is believing in the integrity of our products. Company X, which was about to buy Clif Bar, might have cut ingredient costs. We could make more money using lower-quality ingredients, but that is not our goal as shareholders. A good chef (someone you may not want running your finance department!) looks for the highest-quality ingredients. We have a mass-produced product, but we also look for the best—now organic—ingredients to make a tasty, healthy product. That is our return, not increasing the profit margin at the expense of the ingredients.

We want to be environmentally responsible and continually assess our business's impact on the environment. Many companies deplete natural resources to create short-term profit. As shareholders, a positive return on our investment is the knowledge that we have done what we can to minimize our ecological footprint on the earth. We want to know that we are not madly exploiting the earth's resources and that we

RAISING THE BAR

THE STORY OF CLIF BAR, INC.

are leaving something for future generations to enjoy and cherish.

As sole shareholders we want to create and sustain a business where people can live and experience life, not just where they go to make a living. I always liked working with people. No matter what I did in business, I wanted to create a place where people had fun, worked hard, and felt that their work had meaning. If, at the end of the year, our employees have felt good about coming to work, passionate about the work they do, and have been able to lead balanced lives, we consider that a positive return on our investment.

I might have been able to do great things for the community had I sold the company. But now we have 160 employees who do volunteer work on company time. Clif Bar doesn't just give money; it can also use its resources and organization to give back to the community. At the 2002 end-of-year meeting I told our employees that we have the luxury of self-funding community service and environmental initiatives. That alone is a worthy reason to be in business. For Kit and me, shareholder value is having resources to give to the community that nurtures us.

At the end of the year I want to look at our balance sheet and see that we were good stewards of our business—a company that we are preparing for a long-term future. We choose how we define shareholder value, and we include product integrity, our people, the community, and the earth in the balance sheets. (In Chapter Seven I map out a business model that describes my redefinition of shareholder value in greater detail.)

> **WHY WRITE THIS BOOK?**

This book would never have been written had I sold the company. Over the last few years, as I told my story, people would ask, "So when are you going to write the book?" This book is about the moment when I almost sold the company that I had created and nurtured. It's about defining moments. About making the choice to live with passion, guts, integrity, and values. I hope that readers will be inspired by what Clif Bar has lived through and is living. I hope you learn from our successes and mistakes. By telling the story of my "epiphany ride" I hope to encourage you to follow up on your own ideas. How many people say, "I want to write a book some day," and they continue to say this for thirty years? Or, "I've always thought of starting a restaurant" and they say that for twenty years? So I was on a bike ride. Had an idea.

I hope that there are parts of our business model and redefinition of shareholder value that might work for other companies. What if shareholder value or the bottom line weren't money? Almost selling the company forced me to ask again: *Why does Clif Bar exist? What are our reasons for being?* These two questions shape *Raising the Bar*. By answering these questions for Clif Bar Inc., and for me personally, I hope to answer them for others as well.

Why did I decide to stay private against all "expert" advice? Why does a guy "send them home" and walk away from $60 million? This is the story of why and how.

It's also a story about a bike ride.

CHAPTER 2

THE EPIPHANY RIDE

(THE EARLY YEARS OF CLIF BAR)

Before Clif Bar, every year would find me cycling in European mountains—the Alps, Pyrenees, the Dolomites. On these mega bike trips, my friends and I would cover between one and two thousand miles—most of it over mountain passes. You would also find me rock and mountain climbing, exploring peaks from California's Sierra Nevada range to the Swiss and French Alps. In addition, from 1986 through 1992, I raced bicycles as an amateur road racer. I discovered PowerBar while racing competitively. At that time, PowerBar was the only energy bar on the market. All racers ate these bars, and I started eating them as well. My friends and I carried PowerBars with us on races and on mountain treks. I never thought much about their taste or texture.

Several months after one of our sixteen-hundred-mile bike trips in the Alps, my good friend Jay called to invite me to go with him on a new ride in the San Francisco Bay Area. Jay was always studying maps, devising new rides. He charted out what he hoped would be a great adventure and calculated that we'd cover about 125 miles. We each packed six PowerBars, a banana, and some sports drinks. We left at dawn, cruised up Livermore Valley through Patterson Pass, then nearly thirty miles along the California Aqueduct, then west on a picturesque road named Del Puerto Canyon. As we reached the top of Mount Hamilton we realized that we'd already ridden 120 miles and still had a third of the way to go! Clearly our ride would be much longer than 125 miles, most likely in the 170 mile range. I had eaten five of my six PowerBars. I was exhausted and famished. In cycling they describe what was happening to me as *bonking:* my body was out of fuel and had no more energy. I needed to eat my last PowerBar, yet I suddenly realized that I couldn't choke it down. I just couldn't put it in my mouth. Fortunately our ride from the top of Mount Hamilton was downhill. It was right then, as Jay and I rode down Mount Hamilton, that epiphany number one in the Clif Bar journey hit me. "I think I can make something better than this. Something that if you needed to eat six of them, you wouldn't have to choke the last one down." We ended up riding 175 miles. How did we get home? We hit the nearest 7–Eleven store off Mount Hamilton, where I consumed a six-pack of powdered doughnuts. We rode in the dark, but we made it.

The epiphany ride started everything. What if we had bicycled just a hundred miles and took four PowerBars instead of six? I thank Jay for his outrageous trips and their unknown outcomes. An extreme situation tested me to the point where I needed an alternative to the norm.

Often, for me, the best ideas come out of extreme situations in unknown terrain, whether in cycling or in business. Pushing beyond what I think I can do creates an opening for new ideas.

The bike epiphany was a purely intuitive moment. Yet it brought together three elements of my life in a way that made sense: my passion for cycling, my food sensibility, and my experience running a bakery. At the time, I worked for a bicycle company designing bicycle seats. As a rider and worker in the industry I had watched PowerBar's successful introduction and wide distribution. Every bicycle shop in the nation seemed to carry Power-Bars. All bike racers, including me, ate the bars. I bought them by the box. Yet I had never attempted to eat six in one day.

Bike racers never really complained about the taste of Power-
Bars. We thought they were the bitter pills we needed to swal-
low to help us perform. I accepted this, but I had been brought
up to have a different food sensibility. In my family every
holiday was a Greek food festival. I grew up baking croissants
with my mom. Jay and I had savored fantastic food cycling
through the Alps and the Pyrenees. I didn't want to compromise
on the taste of what I put in my mouth, no matter its purpose.
For me, great cycling and great food didn't need to be separate.

I also co-owned a wholesale business, Kali's Sweets & Savories,
with a friend named Lisa Thomas. Started in Berkeley, California, in 1986, Kali's made delicious cookies and a savory Greek
product called Yoha. My mother created the recipes, and some
of them were adaptations from recipes that my Greek-born
grandmother, Kalliope, had passed down. Our commitment to
taste was the essence of our bakery. We were also beginning
to market and distribute to the natural food industry and to
use organic ingredients in some of our products.

I believe that our epiphanies or intuitive insights often reflect
who we are, or what we are capable of doing, in unexpected
ways. I was a bike racer and consumer of energy bars. I loved
food. I owned a bakery. All the ingredients were there for me;
I just hadn't recognized the combination. I had the skills and

background to manufacture a new product. I believed I could create a bar superior to the only energy bar on the market. The time was right.

Successful entrepreneurs take who they are and what they already know and create surprising combinations.

> ➤ **FROM MOM'S KITCHEN TO LAUNCH**

I called the most creative and expert baker I knew, my mom, and said, "Hey, I'm coming to your house. I want to work on something, and I need your help." I started researching what ingredients were used to make an energy bar. I purchased ingredients and analyzed specification sheets for the existing energy bar. In the process I realized that the energy bar I was studying used highly processed ingredients. The vitamins and minerals had been nearly stripped away. I needed ingredients that were natural and less processed. On the other hand, my mom's cookies tasted great but used lots of butter, white sugar, and oil. I wanted a bar with a nutritional profile similar to PowerBar that used natural ingredients and tasted as good as my mom's cookies. I wanted a bar that tasted great even if it was the sixth bar you ate on a 175-mile bike ride!

My mom and I set out to create an energy bar that tasted good and used all-natural ingredients. We used her cookie recipes and took out the butter. I replaced sugar with naturally processed rice syrup, which contains both complex and simple carbohydrates. We worked on texture. We didn't want a taffy-like, hard, grainy bar like the current energy bar. We asked, "Why couldn't you have nutritional value in a product and still

GARY, MOM (MARY), AND
GRANDMOTHER KALLIOPE.
—CLIFF ERICKSON

RAISING
THE BAR

THE STORY OF CLIF BAR, INC.

" My remembrances of Gary include the fact that instead of a spare tube or tire, he often had rock climbing shoes strapped under his saddle. And a bunch of us went to hear him play his trumpet at a place near Rockridge BART station. He also used to bring his homemade bars on rides for us to try out. While the poor bike racer in me was happy to have some free calories, I remember also thinking that they were pretty darn good. I don't remember the story too clearly now, but I thought he said he had baking in his family, his grandmother, maybe? Anyway, there were some great rides we did fueled on those bars. "

—ERIC ZALTAS, FORMER NATIONAL CHAMPION BIKE RACER

have the same texture as a cookie?" So we started mixing. We
broke paddles. We burned out the motor of her KitchenAid
mixer. Large bags of flour and five gallon buckets of sticky
syrup covered mom's kitchen and pantry. I made a mess of her
pristine kitchen. For six months we mixed, baked, and tossed
out dozens of batches of oats, dried fruit, and all-natural sweeteners. My mom didn't care. She was hanging out with her son
doing something she loved—baking.

SIX MONTHS AFTER THE EPIPHANY RIDE WE
FINALLY "RAISED THE BAR."

How do you get a bar from mom's kitchen into manufacturing?
On the business side, I didn't question that Lisa, the co-owner
of Kali's Bakery, and I continue our fifty-fifty partnership as
Clif Bar became a reality. Our bakery was tiny and we didn't
own the necessary equipment to make the bars. Fortunately
we found a local bakery that could manufacture and pack the
bars. We provided packaging, some of the ingredients, and a
die I designed that created the unique shape of Clif Bar. Still,
it was incredibly difficult to work out the manufacturing. The
bakery we contracted had never produced anything like our
bars, and our dough was so much thicker than cookie dough
that we blew out several motors in their thousand-pound mixers. Fortunately, they graced us with their laughter and concern. And there was a positive side to the difficulties: people
would have a hard time copying us. To date, no one has really
copied Clif Bar.

We couldn't wait to get the new product on the market. Dozens
of friends tested products for me. I started taking bars on bike

RAISING THE BAR

THE STORY OF CLIF BAR, INC.

races, rides, and climbing weekends, giving them to my friends. I swore them to secrecy. Now they ask me, "Do you remember the time you gave me bars in those plain wrappers?" Astonishingly, PowerBar didn't know about Clif until we launched the bar, even though we were in their backyard. We decided to launch the bar at a big bicycle show in September 1991.

It was time to create a design, a package. Even though I had been in business for a long time and had studied business in college, I knew little about branding. I thought about Doug Gilmour, an extraordinarily creative person that I had met while working at a bicycle company. Doug brought art into the business world unlike anyone I had ever met, using his incredible sense of humor and great artistic ability. I told Doug, "I want you to create a package for this product." I didn't have a name. I didn't know what shape the bar would be. I just knew that Doug would "get it." So, after baking my new bar, Doug and I met at Max's Opera House Cafe in San Francisco for our own version of the classic "doodling on a napkin" business story. Doug doodled on a napkin, barely looking at me as I talked, explaining the new bar to him. At one point I looked at what he was sketching and said, "I think you've got it." Doug had drawn a rock climber on a cliff. The essence of the design he created from the napkin sketch remains Clif Bar's package.

GARY BAR FIRST PACKAGE GRAPHIC.
—DOUG GILMOUR

We'd created a bar. We had a package. But we didn't have a name. I wanted a name like PowerBar—something tough and strong. I toyed with names like Forza, the Italian word for strength. I also liked Torque (someone did come out with a bar named torque years later). I envisioned a picture of a bicycle crank. Doug disagreed with my ideas, and, unbeknownst to me, named my product "Gary Bar." When he told me about this, he said, "This has to be personal. This is about your vision, your creation. You are the consumer. You are the bike racer. You tell the story." Somewhat reluctantly I agreed to pursue "Gary Bar." We did a trademark search and found a product called Gary's All Natural Peanuts. We thought, "Well, it's not exactly a bar. Let's write them a letter and tell them what we are doing." In no time flat we received a letter from the large multinational company that made the product telling us that they would come after us with all their attorneys and sue us for so much money that we would regret ever thinking of Gary Bar. We dropped the name. It was mid-summer, and we had a September launch date at an important bike show. This was our big shot at getting the attention of thousands of bike shops, and we still didn't have a name.

Doug and I met regularly in his San Francisco office to work on package design. Just days before the bike show, as I crossed the Bay Bridge to meet Doug, my father's name—Cliff—popped

RAISING THE BAR

" The most vivid memory begins at Max's. The napkin comes out. The drawing. There was a wildly energetic dialogue between Gary and me where we were saying, 'Yes, this is it. This is the direction we want to go.' A few afternoons later in my office I sat down with a relatively new software program and started to draw. My first take wasn't a sketch but a careful drawing of a climber. The reason it didn't have hair was not because Gary was losing it, but because I couldn't draw it. A few days later I showed the initial drawing to Gary and he was dumbfounded, as I was. It had so much energy.

On the shelf there is a homogenization with transnational corporations. There is a tendency toward moving away from the personal. Taking the life out of something and repackaging it as if it has life. The difference is that I want to hold on to the life. "

—DOUG GILMOUR

into my head. Although the package features a cliff, the name had never occurred to me. I wasn't thinking of a mountain cliff, I was thinking of my dad—about how he introduced me to the wilderness and how the package featured an outdoor scene. It grabbed me immediately. I hoped that Doug would like the idea too. Both excited and nervous, I told him, "I've got a name." Doug stared at his computer screen, playing with graphics, not looking at me. I said, "Clif Bar, named after my dad." He still didn't turn to look at me. Instead he slowly started creating a box. He began to shape the words "Clif Bar" using circles, squares, and rectangles. He placed the name exactly where it remains to this day, in Gilmour font. Finally, still without making eye contact, he said, "I like it." And Clif Bar went to market.

Keep it personal. It probably sounds obvious, but I learned to build on my personal passions, my own life experiences and abilities. Do what you know, what you are.

➤ JUST TRY IT!

Clif Bar created a stir at the September 1991 bike show. More than a thousand bike shops expressed interest in our new bar. In February 1992, we formally launched Clif Bar, and within two to three months, seven hundred bike shops carried our product. Clif Bar's almost instant success surprised me. In 1992 we took in $700,000 in annual sales. Clif Bar flew for the next few years, growing exponentially—$1.2 million in annual sales in 1993, $2.2 million the following year. Our growth kept leapfrogging—$5–10 million in 1996 and $10–20 million in annual sales by 1997.

The key to Clif Bar's growth was getting the bars into consumers' mouths. We had no money to market Clif Bar in traditional forms, like an advertising blitz. We took it to the grass roots. I handed out bars to athletes at marathons, bicycle races, climbing competitions, to climbers in Tuolumne Meadows and Yosemite Valley, and I sent dozens of bars to rock climbing buddies, asking them to give them to their friends. We set up booths at sporting events. I remember going to the Boston Marathon. My friend Tad came by the booth to visit and ended up cutting up samples for two days at a pace so fast that we could barely take bathroom breaks!

At first people would walk by our booths without stopping. Maybe they thought that all energy bars tasted the same. I would coax them, "Please, just try it." They would reluctantly grab a piece, walk down the aisle, and stick it in their mouth. Then they would turn around and come back to our booth, surprised and enthusiastic. For years we worked at the grassroots level converting people to our bar. Convincing them to try the bar was the key. With this intensive grassroots approach we made believers out of consumers who thought PowerBar was the only answer for quick and sustained energy.

At first I thought of athletes as our only consumers. Soon a whole new set of consumers emerged: people who shopped in natural food stores. These consumers were looking for a product that was portable, convenient, nutritious, and tasty. Some of the cookies made in the natural foods industry in the 1970s not only looked like the earth, they tasted like dirt. Clif Bar was a product similar to a tasty cookie, yet it was natural

RAISING THE BAR

THE STORY OF CLIF BAR, INC.

and nutritious. Our sales began to grow in the natural food industry. It made sense that in the early years we sold almost exclusively to bike shops and natural food stores. Our consumers in those two venues "got" what we were doing.

Looking back I can see that we were incredibly fortunate in our timing. We were the second major player in the category. As the years went by more competitors entered the field. Today, combining the numerous flavors, brands, and companies on the market, hundreds of nutrition and energy bars exist. Timing can be everything when entering a new market. We had the right bar at the right time.

The key was to get people to taste our bar. An entrepreneur must do whatever it takes to get people to try their new product. That means, as it did in my case, personally giving product to natural consumers in a variety of venues.

Activation Cards with stickers [stamps]

> **FROM GARAGE TO RV**

My personal life changed dramatically in the first few years after launching Clif Bar. In 1994 I was thirty-seven, and my mom was still wondering if I would ever get married, much less have children. A year later I had three children, two from my wife's previous marriage (I tell the love story in Chapter Five).

I wasn't living in a garage, hanging out with friends, driving my old Datsun 510 to Yosemite to go climbing. I was living in my in-laws' recreational vehicle with my wife, three children, and a dog! My mom's wish had come true, sort of. The reality of us living in a RV that was parked in front of the house we were building probably didn't match her dream, or how she thought I'd attain it. I wasn't making enough money from Clif Bar to afford to build my own house, but there was the hole in the ground! I guess that's living on faith. My life might have seemed more complicated, but it felt right. I remember I'd wake up at 6 A.M., cut tile for the house steps, get the kids ready for school at 7:30, wash up in the RV sink, and put on a suit and tie to go to court. To court? Putting on a suit and tie to go to court had not been part of my plans, but we'd been sued.

➤ DON'T KILL THE LAWYERS

Although we couldn't afford to advertise much, we did create one ad for our big launch. We wanted to make our mark and differentiate ourselves from our main competitor. Doug and I created a print advertisement that read, "It's your body. You decide." The advertisement featured a photograph of the ingredients used in Clif Bar alongside a list of the ingredients used in PowerBar, making visual the stark difference between Power-Bar's highly processed white powders and chemical-looking

RAISING THE BAR

THE STORY OF CLIF BAR, INC.

syrups and Clif Bar's whole grains, fruits, and natural sweeteners. Two days later PowerBar sued, claiming we misrepresented their product. They demanded $300,000—this before we'd sold a single bar! Since we'd photographed the actual list of ingredients, they didn't prevail, and we settled for the token sum of $5,000.

Another issue that got us involved with lawyers was distribution. We decided to use master distributors to launch the product, one for sport and bike outlets and another for the natural food industry. The sport distributor happened to be the same company that had employed me earlier. Both distributors did fine at first. One distributor, however, was unable to pay us for product and both wanted a bigger and bigger piece of Clif Bar. Their performance was also weakening and I felt the business would flatten if we didn't wrest control away from our distributors and operate in-house. But I'd made a huge mistake: Naively, I had entered major distribution agreements with handshake deals. I had given them too much control and now had no legal agreement to back up our position. We settled one relationship for under $100,000. I ended up in court with the other distributor, the bike company. We settled for $1.9 million, including attorneys' fees. Severing these ties cost us close to $2 million at a time when our annual sales were just over $2 million.

I want to encourage entrepreneurs to use legal counsel from day one. Over the years I've known many people starting new companies who shied away from hiring an attorney because they thought that they couldn't afford the fees. I know from sad experience that one three-hour meeting can save you a million dollars down the road. I've come to depend on legal counsel and trust it.

> **RIDING THE WAVE**

Wow—what a ride. This amazingly passionate, iconoclastic company. The key to Clif Bar's success thus far is its spirit. It is a spirit that's fueled by an idealism that is adopted by every new member of this ever-expanding family.

—CLIF BAR EMPLOYEE

In the fall of 1994 we brought distribution in-house. Now Lisa, our two employees, and I were doing everything, literally. There wasn't any aspect of the business that we didn't touch. Within any given twenty-four-hour period I might be developing a new Clif Bar flavor or sweeping the floors (or both). This business model differs quite a bit from the model used by new companies that start with venture capital funding. We had to do everything ourselves; they usually have the luxury of starting with a full staff.

We need to get to the races ...

" I went down there and it was just a tiny little warehouse bay with one small office space. Gary didn't have a place for me. He handed me a stack of papers to get organized. I actually took them home to work on because there was no computer for me. When the second bay opened, I set up a desk there, literally in the warehouse. I began in November so I started to provide product to winter sports events. I would call up a promoter for a cross-country ski race and say, 'Hey, we have this Clif Bar, this natural energy bar. It is a fantastic product. We would like to donate product to your race and get it out to the athletes. Perhaps you could put up a banner or something for us at the race.' (We sent out nylon banners to events and asked people to send them back because we only had six.) They would say, 'Huh? Why are you trying to give me this product?' I would have to beg them to take the product because they had never heard of it and didn't know what it was. And then the forklift would pass behind me and it was real echoey and the guy on the other end would say, 'It sounds like you are in a warehouse or something.' And I would say, 'Well, I *am* in a warehouse.' Obviously the already dubious proposition now sounded even dicier. He has never heard of this product. It is a small company. Some guy is calling him from a noisy warehouse. And he is wondering, 'What is this?'

So I really had to push to get the product into those events. Eventually it happened. It was strictly a grassroots, seat-of-the-pants athlete and event sponsorship effort. It went from that stack of papers to an organized grassroots marketing program. It was really small time but we were passionate about it. "

—PAUL MCKENZIE, DIRECTOR OF LUNA CHIX,
   FORMERLY DIRECTOR OF MARKETING AND CREATIVE SERVICES

We depended on grassroots marketing, and I wanted to crank up this side of the business. Up until 1995 I did the grassroots marketing alone. I found all the sporting and natural food events. I solicited all the athletes we sponsored. In 1995, I hired my good friend Paul McKenzie and handed him a large stack of papers with the names of all the people and events we sponsored, saying, "Take it. Develop the grassroots marketing program." He did that and more. Paul worked with magazines, advertising, photography, athletes, sponsors, and soon grew an entire department. Paul's entrepreneurial spirit symbolized how we worked in those early Clif Bar days. Seeds were planted and grew.

Clif Bar was on a mission. We flew for the next few years, growing from $2 million to $5 million, $5 million to $10 million, and $10 million to $20 million in annual sales. Every aspect of the business kept growing. Clif Bar Inc. started with three people, then five, then seven. We desperately needed employees— operations people, shipping people, marketers, salespeople. It became humorous. Our standing joke was that if someone walked by the office and seemed to be breathing, we would yank them in, hand them a phone, and tell them to start fielding calls. Fortunately, we found great people by applying the "you can walk and breathe" criterion, many of whom remain with Clif Bar to this day.

Tiny warehouse units housed Clif Bar during the early years. They were cold and damp in the winter and were prone to flooding, given our proximity to the bay (a serious problem for a company that stored a food product!). Paul and I had offices in the warehouse. A high school friend of mine's "office" consisted of a desk under a pallet rack. The work was so constant that I actually lived in the warehouse for a few weeks, setting up a temporary home: a couch for sleeping, a television, and a makeshift kitchen. People arrived at work in the morning as I struggled to get out of bed (or couch) after working late into the night.

I continued to develop new flavors, eventually adding ten new flavors to our original three. We were the first to make chocolate chip bars, chocolate espresso, and carrot cake. We still introduce one or two new flavors every year. We became known as innovators in the energy bar food category and our flavors were often imitated.

In 1997 we introduced Clif Shot, another sport-oriented product. Designed to compete directly with Gu, Clif Shot is a liquid product used by athletes for quick energy. During long endurance events chewing can be difficult—liquid Clif Shot is absorbed more quickly than solids. We entered the market with a natural version, which set us apart from similar products that used preservatives and highly processed ingredients. Clif Shot quickly became a strong player in the category.

Clif Bar kept innovating and growing.

> ➤ **THE CLIF SPIRIT**
> There is a fire here that is good and strong and burns brightly.
> **—CLIF BAR EMPLOYEE**

It was fun to work at Clif Bar in the early years. We were a small, fast-growing business with cool brands and high-quality, healthy products. It was fun selling a product consumers were

PAUL McKENZIE IN WAREHOUSE OFFICE
("DRAMATIC" REENACTMENT).
—JENI ROGERS

RAISING THE BAR

THE STORY OF CLIF BAR, INC.

" I went to Clif Bar in the early days and met with the operations manager of the warehouse. She said, 'You're hired.' We had a little bay warehouse with a tiny front office. Six people shared four computers. We were growing so fast that the equipment and the manpower couldn't catch up with the work. I remember that to answer one of the phones you had to pull the phone cord around the backs of other people. It was really busy and everybody had to pitch in and do everything. Everyone packed boxes. Everyone answered the phone. In traditional Clif Bar style we started parties in the parking lot. Gary was funny and rolled with it. "

—CASSIE CYPHERS, CLIF BAR EMPLOYEE

excited about. Creating grassroots events was exciting. Even shipping out a bunch of product was fun. Our warehouse units were so small that we packaged and loaded in the parking lot! We didn't have loading docks, so when trucks arrived we pulled pallets out one at a time using a long chain. Product to be delivered often sat in the parking lot. During the winter, when it rains a lot in northern California, mounds of pallets covered in blue plastic tarp dotted our parking lot—mounds that represented thousands and thousands of dollars worth of inventory. We were flying by the seat of our pants and employees loved it. Maybe employees recognized the passion that the owners had for the work. Maybe they sensed a deeper meaning. Maybe they sensed that Clif Bar was different. Clif Bar attracted people who wanted to be part of the vision, people who got it.

Clif Bar athletes also got it. We needed athletes to represent our product and to talk about Clif Bar with other athletes. We looked for athletes who lived for more than the finish line. Our contract with athletes actually stated that all of life should be enjoyed, that life is not only about the finish line. We would rather sponsor someone who comes in second place and is humble than an arrogant first-place winner. Of course we wanted the athletes to perform well, even win races, but we stressed that Clif Bar believed that the fun of getting there is getting there. We looked for athletes who were friendly, hardworking, fun, and above all, not arrogant.

Over the years our core sports have been running, triathlon, cycling (both road and mountain), rock climbing, skiing, and snowboarding. These sports are about endurance, about the individual; they're human-powered sports. In the early years we sought out 80 percent of our athletes and 20 percent approached us. Currently we don't solicit athletes or events. When athletes or athletic events solicit us, we apply the same criteria as before: humility, joy, hard work, and the belief that life is not about the finish line.

When I was young I worked in a ski shop, which was very cool because I loved to ski. Later I parked cars, waited tables, hammered nails, roamed the Sierra as a mountain guide, and played my horn in various bands. Then I worked in the bicycle industry, which was great because I loved to ride and race. Now at Clif Bar I was making a product that fed athletes that participated in the sports I loved—cycling, skiing, running, rock climbing. I met incredible people, many of them top athletes. I raced mountain bikes with people in the company. I loved food and got to create food as my job. I loved manufacturing. I loved being on the line. I loved working on new products. I worked with great people, doing things that I loved: *I had my dream job.*

➤ GROWING PAINS

Clif Bar is a great company whose growing pains have caused much stress among employees.
The shifting sands beneath one's feet.
What will happen next?
—CLIF BAR EMPLOYEE, FALL 1998

We were blessed with early success and rapid growth, with happy consumers and wonderful employees who shared the Clif vision, but with rapid growth came constant change and growing

CLIF BAR GROWTH CHART

SALES HISTORY

Year	Annual Sales
1992	$700,000
1993	$1,250,000
1994	$2,500,000
1995	$5,200,000
1996	$10,000,000
1997	$20,000,000
1998	$30,000,000
1999	$39,000,000
2000	$68,000,000
2001	$88,000,000
2002	$106,000,000

RAISING
THE BAR

THE STORY OF CLIF BAR, INC.

I sometimes slept outside in my car after working two shifts. I'd wake up at 4:AM and start another two shifts.

pains. All was not always well in Clifland. We faced growing pains in all aspects of the business, including manufacturing. In the first month we made thirty thousand bars, which was more cookies than Kali's Sweets and Savories ever made in a year. Later we made up to a million bars in a single day. Quality and process issues became extremely important. We subcontracted production and didn't own the bakeries. Yet for the first seven years, I spent nearly every day of production on the line. I sometimes slept outside the bakery in my car after working two shifts. I'd wake up at four in the morning and start another two shifts. I was always looking for the best process and striving for the highest quality. I felt like a chef who couldn't leave the kitchen.

With the pressures of rapid growth, a division of labor developed between Lisa and me. I had a background in manufacturing and I developed the bar; I knew industrial engineering. I spent time conducting research, developing products, and monitoring quality control issues on the line. Lisa also spent time on the line and managed other aspects of the business, particularly finance. I was a perfectionist when it came to quality issues. I also had ideas for the manufacturing process itself. At times our rapid growth strained relations with our manufacturers. We became the major product or largest percentage of business for some plants, further complicating relationships.

Growing beyond our natural market changed our business even more. Grocery channels approached us about carrying Clif products. This signified that demand had expanded beyond natural food and bicycle and outdoor sports. It also meant that we were clearly competing against large companies. Supporting new channels of distribution was complicated and expensive.

Some bicycle and outdoor and natural food stores expressed dis-
appointment as we left our earlier niches. We believed that we
needed to listen to the natural demand for our product. People
bought Ben & Jerry's ice cream in both convenience and natural
food stores. We wanted to make Clif Bars similarly available.

We were changing because we were growing exponentially and
frantically trying to catch up. Clif was now officially a national
brand, not just a small, quirky Berkeley company, and we worried that our identity would change.

*Any company that is growing will have growing pains. How you
deal with the stresses will determine if your company moves
from adolescence to healthy adulthood.*

➤ BEGINNING TO DRIFT

I am a little bit lost. There is a lot of confusion around. Now it
seems like everything is starting to go crazy. When I started
I was the fifteenth employee. I wonder how we can survive to be
that once cool little company we were a few years ago.

—CLIF BAR EMPLOYEE, FALL 1998

We began to drift in 1998, losing some of the essence of what
made Clif Bar a special place to work. Things change when you
grow from three employees to fifty, then to a hundred. You need
to develop policies and procedures. You bring in people who
may not fit. Many had worked with other companies, both large
and small, and wanted to conduct business the way it had been
done at their previous employers. Young workers with little work
experience entered Clif Bar with the world by the tail, certain of

how things should be done. We started to see a shift in employee attitude and spirit. Employees who had been with the company were saying, "It is so different now. Where are we going?" Some used the term "drifting boat" to describe Clif Bar Inc.

Gossip became prevalent—in the hallways and on e-mail. People gossiped about the owners, middle-level management, each other. Gossip is a sign of a dysfunctional environment. I felt horrible and oppressed by employee issues. I just wanted everyone to be respectful of each other and continue with the camaraderie of the early years. On a company off-site retreat, two facilitators, Lanny Vincent and Jim Armstrong, led us through writing exercises, including poetry. We sat outside in a beautiful park, and they encouraged people to write about their experiences with and feelings about Clif Bar. "What was the essence of Clif Bar? What did Clif Bar mean to them?" Although most employees wrote about their commitment to Clif Bar and how glad they were to be working at the company, problems surfaced as well. One person wrote, "Clif Bar is growing so fast that we don't have time to think about whether we are doing the job right or wrong, just about getting the job done." Sitting in the park watching people write, I realized, "This is really getting harder." I realized that with so much growth, all the new people that I barely knew, diverse feelings and attitudes, it would continue to be difficult.

I was starting to feel burdened by the company that I loved with a passion.

Employee morale progressively worsened. We hired other mediators and consultants. The following year, a small upper-management group tried to develop a mission and values statement for the company. We went off-site and developed a lofty statement without involving the majority of the people in the process. We delivered the statement at an all-company meeting in 1999, and it elicited negative reactions, not the positive responses we hoped for.

The lesson I learned was that at whatever level possible, tell your people what you are doing as you develop company mission and value statements and ask for their ideas and feedback. Clif Bar employees had strong feelings about our mission, values, and direction. We weren't listening. If employees don't feel that they shape the mission of the company, they will become resentful. Even with thousands of employees, company mission statements should express employee values and aspirations.

Despite the growing pains, annual sales grew an amazing 50 percent from 1997 to 1998. In August 1998 Lisa surprised me by announcing that she wanted out. The stress of competing against PowerBar and Balance Bar and the pressures created

RAISING THE BAR

THE STORY OF CLIF BAR, INC.

by our own rapid growth were weighing her down. She feared losing it all. I tried to be sympathetic to her fears. The stress was understandable given our growing pains. I attempted to explain how I visualized what was happening at Clif Bar using a climbing metaphor. I told her to imagine that we were climbing Mount Everest very successfully. We arrive at Camp Four, one camp before the top, and in rolls a storm. We hunker down in the tent to wait until the storm blows over. "That is where we are with Clif Bar," I told her. "There are growing pains but we are successful. We just need to get through this storm. Then we will unzip the tent door, walk outside on a clear day, look up and see the summit." The only option to waiting out the storm would be radical—a high altitude helicopter rescue. Asking for a rescue as a 50 percent partner would drastically affect the company's chances of summiting or being successful. Through our discussions at this time I realized that my partner and I had dramatically different visions for the company. I wanted to ride out the storm. My partner wanted the helicopter ride.

Lisa decided to stay with Clif Bar after a month-long trip that gave her time to reflect. We knew, however, that the nature of our partnership had to change. Since the beginnings of Clif Bar we had shared the title of CEO. Now, although we still shared core values, the tension between us would only worsen if we remained co-CEOs. I figured out a possible solution and suggested that Lisa become the CEO of Clif Bar. This might surprise you since she initially wanted the helicopter ride out of the company. Since she now wanted to run the company, I decided to ride out the storm. I took a back seat, focusing on things I could do that I thought would help the company. By

early 1999 Lisa was running day-to-day operations at Clif Bar
Inc. I focused on research and development. I also took up a
new distraction, golf, spending time on the links to give my
partner space to run the company. In retrospect I can see how
much I was detaching. My passion for Clif Bar remained, even
if I couldn't figure out how I fit in the Clif picture. Oddly enough,
1999, one of our hardest years internally, was also the year of
one of our greatest business triumphs.

➤ SHOOTING FOR THE LUNA

In 1998 we were looking for a new product and brand. We
tested ideas, listened to our consumers at events, and paid careful attention to consumer service calls. Women who cared about
their health told us they needed an energy bar more geared to
their lifestyle. They wanted a bar lower in calories and with
ingredients essential to women, such as calcium, iron, and folic
acid. We responded and created the Luna Bar. I jumped into
the kitchen and developed the first four flavors in three days. I
held internal focus groups with women at Clif Bar, who helped
me refine Nuts over Chocolate, Lemon Zest, Toasted Nuts and
Cranberries, and Chocolate Pecan Pie Luna Bars. Luna Bars
are lighter, with a crispier texture than Clif Bars, and they
have fewer calories. Inspired by women at Clif Bar, Doug over-
saw the creative side, designing the package and selecting the
name. Sheryl O'Loughlin, chief of brand, orchestrated the
launch. Industry experts told us that we were giving up half
our market (men) by going after women. National Public Radio
even ran a story on the Luna Bar in which business analysts
questioned the wisdom of "giving up" half the market. Yet

RAISING THE BAR

THE STORY OF CLIF BAR, INC.

RAISING THE BAR

THE STORY OF CLIF BAR, INC.

" The introduction of Luna was a dream come true. It felt like we were in 'the zone' as all the brand pieces started coming together. At the time, the concept of a bar for women was new, risky, and just what the marketplace needed. Women were begging for a product with a nutritional profile just for women and less calories than most other bars. Also, with a delicate, crisp texture and more decadent taste. No company was listening. Conventional wisdom said that women just don't use energy bars because, at the time, 70 percent of the category was used by men. We started asking why instead of assuming that that's just the way it is.

We had push-back during the initial introduction phase. Other companies, some retailers, and various members of the press were saying, 'What are you thinking?' In their minds the positioning was cutting off half the population. Despite the resistance, we had the courage to keep an intense focus on the consumer—the ultimate user of the product. We kept at it with passion. That's the beautiful thing with *natural demand,* the consumer proved that it should be on the shelf and now it is the number one bar.

Sometimes you have to fight against conventional wisdom because conventional wisdom is always going to go with the path of least resistance. With the known. If you go with the logic that everyone knows; you will produce the same thing as everyone else. And someone who takes a little bit of a maverick approach and does it right will make a difference. "

–SHERYL O'LOUGHLIN, CHIEF OF BRAND

Could
I start a glove line for
runners. an cyclist who live
and train in cold environments..
~~Training t-shirts~~ → that can
be sent to athletes,
long white semi tight...

Sheryl knew we had something big with Luna. She was right.
We projected $1.5 million in sales the first year and ended up
with $10 million. We easily could have sold $12 million but our
contract bakery was not prepared to produce more than six
times the amount we had projected. We had thought we would
hit a single and ended up with a home run.

Luna's surprising success occurred with less than $200,000 in
advertising. As I wrote earlier, we've never really been big on
traditional advertising. Most large companies would never
accept a sales projection as low as $1.5 million for a new prod-
uct. And most companies would put $20–40 million into a brand
launch. We don't have that kind of money because we're self-
funded. We go out slow and see what kind of product we have.
Luna flew off the shelves in bicycle and outdoor stores, which
genuinely surprised us. We created Clif Bar as the energy bar
and Luna as the nutrition bar for women. Yet, after only three
years, Luna bars were outselling our original Clif Bar line.
And, contrary to the experts, Luna found a niche among men
too. It's unprecedented for a second brand to beat a successful
first brand, but Luna did.

Launching Luna brought a lot of excitement into the company.
Almost all of the women at Clif Bar participated in the process
of creating Luna.

RAISING THE BAR

THE STORY OF CLIF BAR, INC.

Luna taught us that listening to the experts might not lead to success. Women told us they wanted a bar geared to women's needs. We believed them. At Clif Bar we try to follow natural demand rather than create demand.

➤ ALMOST SELLING

Clif Bar became a dominant player in both the health food and energy bar worlds. In 1999 we hit $40 million in annual sales, which meant we were catching up to PowerBar. We made the Inc. 500—*Inc.* magazine's list of the nation's fastest-growing privately held companies—four years running. We still had not taken on any outside capital. Growing without taking on outside capital was a source of pride to me. People wanted to invest in Clif Bar all the time. I kept saying no. Venture capitalists and funders who wanted to invest money with us tempted my business partner and others at Clif Bar. From 1998 until we nearly sold the company, the continual refrain from many in the company was "we need funding to grow." People became convinced that the only way Clif Bar Inc. could survive was through an infusion of capital from outside the company.

I didn't get it. Maybe I was just naive. We were already growing and consistently profitable. How would external funding be different? I was told that a big company could bring us added distribution power, increase our manufacturing capacity, save us money on ingredients, help us develop products, and so on and so on. If we joined up with a big company they could take us to the next level. So I went along for the ride. Stress related to my business partnership and the voice of conventional wisdom affected my decision making. I ignored the fact that I was fine with our current growth rate. I didn't listen to the voice inside that was telling me that the drive to go "to the next level" seemed like *growth for growth's sake rather than growth to further a vision.*

We agreed that Lisa would take on the task of finding strategic alliances or joint ventures as a means of obtaining funding to grow the company. When Mars Inc., one of the largest privately held companies in the world, approached us I felt flattered. Mars wanted a minority position in Clif Bar. It also wanted an exit strategy, including the right to buy Clif Bar in five years. Who could blame anyone for that? Yet it was hard for me to accept. It meant that if Mars invested a lot of money and helped grow the company and everything went well, it would gain the right to buy the rest of the company. If all didn't go as planned, we were in trouble. In spite of my misgivings, I consented to pursuing this option in early 2000.

Just as we were ready to negotiate with Mars for minority equity, Balance Bar sold to Kraft. A few weeks later Nestlé bought PowerBar. Now "funding to grow" had new meaning for the company. The refrain became "do or die." Investment bankers, my business partner, and conventional wisdom claimed that the "big guys" would work hard to marginalize us. They believed that unless we grew rapidly Clif Bar Inc. would die. Inviting Mars in as a minority shareholder looked different in that context. I realized, "I can't do this." Even though I respected Mars as a company, I didn't want another partner and the timing was not right for Mars for a full acquisition. It became an either/or situation for me: Either stay private and continue growing through self-funding or sell the whole thing.

RAISING THE BAR

THE STORY OF CLIF BAR, INC.

If the only way to continue growing the company was to bring in a partner and thus lose the freedom we had as a privately held company, I wasn't interested. I would rather sell. Yet, I believed we could still survive as a privately held company. In January 2000 I called my partner and explained the either/or situation. The first words out of her mouth were, "I want to sell the company." I said, "OK, let's do it."

We told key people in the company about our decision to sell. We hired an investment banker to broker the deal. We told friends and family. Ironically, I dove headfirst back into the company to prepare it for sale. We told employees to gear up for the sale. We asked people to work harder than they ever had to help us prepare to sell Clif Bar Inc. We promised everyone that they would receive generous bonuses at the end of the trail. If Clif employees would not be able to retire to tropical paradises, at least the bonuses would ease the pain. Even so, I had trouble looking people in the eyes during this process. I went into what I call my "paramedic" mode. I couldn't feel. I couldn't see the blood. I just had to get the job done quickly.

The process of selling a company through investment bankers is an incredible experience. It is calculated and orchestrated. It is about who you know. About who you talked to when. It is fast. It is about wheeling and dealing, wining and dining.

" We saw a bunch of suits around the office so we knew something was happening. But there were rumors, people saying, 'They are going to sell the company, I'm going to be out of a job. As soon as we are bought everyone will get fired.' I saw them go into meetings all the time. Groups of people in business suits. It was funny because no one is ever here in a suit. "

— CLIF BAR EMPLOYEE

" We are constantly being told that Clif Bar is looking for external sources of financing to help us grow, but otherwise we are being kept in the dark. The current activity regarding PowerBar and Balance Bar is creating a lot of concern as to how long it will take the big money from Nestlé and Kraft to squeeze us out of the energy bar market. "

— CLIF BAR EMPLOYEE

In the end, however, selling becomes just about money. I know a few companies and people who negotiated good deals that enabled them to save some company values. Still, they no longer control the destiny of their companies. From what I've seen, many pioneers in the socially responsible business arena (and others) would do it differently now.

Every March we exhibit at the Natural Products Expo West in Anaheim, California, to display our company and introduce new products. We showed up in 2000 as if nothing was going on at Clif Bar. Yet everyone knew that Clif Bar was "on the block." The whole experience was particularly poignant for me that year because my mom and dad attended. They were so proud of me and of the company. People met them for the first time. Yet there was also this buzz about the sale. Following the Expo I usually went to Baja California with a group of friends to play golf, eat seafood, and hang out. This year I told my friend Steve that I couldn't make it because "there was too much going on." Halfway through the show I realized I desperately needed a break so I went to Baja. I didn't talk to my friends about what was happening at Clif Bar. Finally, as we were preparing to leave, I asked them questions, "Do you think Clif Bar can make it? Do you think we can compete? What would you do in my shoes?" They challenged me. Their collective message was, "Sell the company if you want. But do it because you feel it is the right thing to do. Don't use the big company competition as an excuse. You have the best products in the industry. You can compete." They called my bluff. I knew they were right, but I went right back into the process of selling Clif Bar Inc.

➤ THE WALK

Five companies were bidding for Clif Bar Inc. In the thick of the negotiations, I went with my wife, son, and a friend to opening day for the Giants at Pacific Bell (PacBell) Park in San Francisco. There I was at this incredible celebration, totally preoccupied. Lisa was telling me via cell phone about the bids and the incredible amount of money two companies were willing to pay for Clif Bar. I was with my family watching my favorite team play in an incredible new stadium, in a city I love, and I had just been told I was about to become a very rich man. Yet I didn't jump for joy. By this point, selling Clif Bar Inc. seemed inevitable to me. The big guys would eat us up. The company might go under. Employees had worked furiously for months preparing for this sale.

ON APRIL 17, 2000, WE PREPARED TO MEET BANKERS, ATTORNEYS, AND REPRESENTATIVES FROM COMPANY X. I TOOK A WALK. WE DIDN'T SIGN. WE DIDN'T SELL.

RAISING THE BAR

THE STORY OF CLIF BAR, INC.

CHAPTER 3

A DRIFTING BOAT

(GETTING CLIF BACK ON COURSE)

Imagine the company the day after I decided not to sell. My business partner and I had convinced our employees that Clif Bar had to be sold in order to continue to exist. We'd told everyone that the company couldn't compete with giants like Nestlé and Kraft. Employees had exhausted themselves readying Clif Bar for sale. Then we didn't sell. Now it looked like the CEO was about to resign. Clif Bar Inc. was a boat with a hole in its side and the skipper was about to take the only lifeboat and half the supplies. *What could I do?*

> **THE END OF A FIFTY-FIFTY PARTNERSHIP**

When we took the company off the market, my partner and I had a handshake agreement that we would continue as a private company but that she needed a nest egg of $10 million to relieve her stress over the uncertain future. After all, I had taken $120 million off the table. We agreed to look for a bank loan to make this possible. I wanted my partner to stay the course. I wanted us to run the company together. It was not to be.

Within three days of deciding not to sell Clif Bar, Lisa e-mailed me a long letter. She outlined our options: maintain the status quo, which meant staying private and self-funded; form a strategic alliance with a larger company; or sell (two companies from the original bidding remained interested). Lisa still wanted to sell the company. In another message she wrote, "After a lot of thinking I still come out feeling very nervous about our ability to compete and stay healthy without selling or aligning with a big company. I know that you and I share very similar dreams and desires. The difference is, and it is a big and crucial difference, I am not comfortable taking on any more risk."

Two days later, my partner resigned as CEO. We agreed that I would take over as CEO. She sent e-mail to Clif employees announcing that we were taking the company off the market, that she was resigning, and that I would become the new CEO. Employees didn't know what to think. The day I walked into Clif Bar as the new CEO, only one person congratulated me.

Others stared at me with "Who are you?" looks. Later many employees told me they had thought I wouldn't last long,

We made a big mistake in announcing such dramatic events and changes in the company over e-mail. David Pottruck, the CEO of Charles Schwab, says that you have to earn the right to use e-mail. You have to spend a lot of time with people individually and in front of people as a company before they will allow you to deliver news through e-mail. We hadn't won that right.

Lisa went to a cabin we owned together on the east side of the Sierra Nevada. We both needed time apart to reflect on what we wanted for ourselves and for the company. From the moment of my parking lot epiphany I was clear about one thing: I wanted Clif Bar to continue, privately held, no external funding. As I wrote to her on April 22, 2000, "I need to be able to focus 99 percent of my energy and attention on healing wounds, focusing people on moving forward, boosting morale and growing the business. The company cannot afford anything else or anything unusual right now." Two days later she wrote to me from the Sierra, "I realize that I want to get out of this. I've seen my glory days at Clif Bar, and I am ready to move on."

Her decision meant that "unusual" hit me right on the head. My partner wanted out. I offered to pay $25 million (this from a guy with $10,000 in his bank account) and asked her to remain a minority shareholder for the long haul. I figured Clif Bar could handle the $25 million and I hoped that the new amount would help her feel secure. She refused and demanded that I buy her out completely within a five-year period. My partner wanted all her money out of the company. There was no negotiation over this basic point, and she threatened to dissolve the company if she didn't get what she wanted. Dissolving the company would have been Armageddon, the end of Clif Bar Inc. We had to work our way toward an agreement through our attorneys. Negotiations lasted for seven months.

I needed roughly $50 million to satisfy her demand. I would need another $30 million to cover finance costs, if I was lucky. How could I possibly pay her $50 million plus financing to the combined tune of $80 million? How could I grow the company at the same time? The risk for me and for Clif Bar increased tenfold. I felt like a climber wearing lead boots in a whiteout. By this point, however, nothing was going to stop me.

First I tried to get a bank loan and discovered that it is extremely difficult to find non-equity money. Money for this purpose is referred to as "redemption of stock" or "recapitalization." It means an ownership change. In our case, one of the owners wanted to cash out, and banks are reluctant to loan money for the purpose of buying out a partner. A bank would rather loan money to grow a business. I also learned that we didn't have the financial history, the profit, or the assets to get a loan even close to the amount I needed.

Clif faced a double hit. Everyone had told us, "You need money to grow." Now we not only had to grow without outside funding, but Clif Bar Inc. needed a big loan that would be used to pay off a partner rather than grow the company. We struck out

RAISING
THE
BAR

THE STORY OF CLIF BAR, INC.

again and again. No bank would loan us even $10 million, and
I needed $50 million!

Since banks refused to lend us money, I looked into what is
called "mezzanine funding." In mezzanine funding, lenders take
a higher risk but also demand a higher return. Interest rates
range from 20 percent to 25 percent compounded annually. Or
the percentage might be 20 percent along with a minority ownership of the company. Let's say that a mezzanine funder takes
1 percent, 2 percent, or 3 percent of the company. If you successfully grow, five years later the 3 percent will be worth much
more. Yet I struck out with mezzanine lenders also.

My goal was to own and control Clif Bar 100 percent. The
thought of another partner made me ill, yet, due to our volatile
situation, I entered into negotiations with a venture capital
group. The process felt eerily similar to the process of selling
the company. Again it began with the soft sell: "This is an amazing company. We really love you. We can help you grow. We
want to invest in Clif Bar." Again, the advantages were obvious:
The venture capital group would invest some of their money
and enable us to secure a bank loan. I could get the money I
needed to pay off my partner and take control of the company.
But again, it was incredibly expensive money. The venture capital group required a 35 percent return on their investment,

Invest
VC Money

compounded annually. Thus, an initial $12 million investment
would become, five years later, a $50 million bill due in its
entirety (the group's contract stipulated that I could not pay off
the investment early). Combine this with what Clif would owe
to the bank and Lisa, and the bill could be well over $120 mil-
lion. If the money weren't bad enough, the venture capital
group demanded an excessive level of management control.
The two-page sign-off document required a consensus on salaries, compensation, new product launches, and the annual
budget, to name just a few of the stipulations. Moreover, selling
the company five years out was their primary goal. So I risked
having to sell the company if I couldn't pay the $50 million de-
manded by the venture capital group. Finally, for $12 million,
the venture capital group demanded 30 percent ownership of
the company.

If my dream of 100 percent ownership were to come true, I'd
need around $120 million at the end of five years. Even if I could
do that, I'd be forced to give up 30 percent of common stock to
the venture capital group. For me, losing control of the company
was the worst. In the end I walked away from the deal. I sent
them home too.

Back to the drawing board. No bank would lend us the money.
Investment from a venture capital group wouldn't work. My

business partner still wanted her money, but she was willing to negotiate again, through our attorneys. We finally ended up agreeing to a payment of $15 million up front, with another $42 million owed in five years, plus $1 million a year under a noncompete agreement. Clif went bank shopping again and finally made a deal. The bank loaned us enough, at mezzanine rates (23 percent, which included 3 percent of the company in phantom stock), to give my partner $15 million up front with the remainder of what was owed to her held in Series A common stock at a fixed value plus interest.

On October 31, 2000, we signed the new agreement. My partner walked away with a total of $62 million over the next five years. I walked away owning 67 percent of the company; I wouldn't be 100 percent owner until I paid Lisa in full. Yet I dropped to last place in terms of financial security. If any liquidation of the company occurred, I would be last in line to receive money. The whole world changed for the company and me. Big questions remained. Could Clif Bar Inc. pay this enormous debt? How many years would it take? Could we pay our debt without taking on another equity partner or financing that would choke us?

My attorney Bruce Lymburn guided me through many difficult moments in the process and finessed me through a volatile period. At every fork in the road, Bruce gave me the perspective that I needed and the legal counsel that allowed me to save the company. At one point during the seven months leading up to the agreement with my partner, the investment banker who headed up the deal to sell Clif Bar flew out from Chicago to have lunch with Bruce. He wanted Bruce to persuade me to change my mind. According to Bruce the investment banker

THE LAWYER'S STORY

" I was leaving a meeting near San Francisco's Union Square when my cell phone rang. It was Gary, who was sitting with Lisa in a bar in Berkeley. 'We just walked away from $120 million,' he said. 'I can't believe it. Lisa's having a martini. Did we do the right thing? What will we do now?'

On that beautiful spring morning in 2000 I sat on a bench in Union Square and spoke with Gary and Lisa for a long time. I tried to be supportive. 'Good for you,' I said. 'You made the right choice.' I tried to put conviction in my voice, but I'm not sure that I was persuasive. But in any event the decision had been made and there was no going back. I'm not sure that I would have had the courage to walk away from $120 million, but since Gary and Lisa had done it, I hoped that they knew what they were doing.

Thus began an amazing phase of my journey as an attorney for Clif Bar and Gary Erickson. Over the next seven months and beyond, Wendel, Rosen and I (hopefully) played a helpful role in one of the most fascinating transactions I have ever experienced in my career as a business lawyer. I believe that the key to any successful business transaction is to identify what the opposing parties want, and to give those things to each of them in some meaningful way. This is especially true where the bargaining power of both sides is about equal. To create a successful transaction, the parties must create a win-win outcome—the parties must both get what they want and need.

Gary's buy-out of Lisa is a story of hopes of fortunes won and fears of fortunes lost, of faith in the future and fear of the future, of relationships continuing and ended.

For me, my journey with Gary and Clif Bar continues to be a rewarding one. Inspired by Clif Bar's model of corporate governance, in 2003 Wendel, Rosen, Black & Dean became the first law firm in the country to be certified as a 'green business,' with environmental sustainability as a core value. Our journey continues. "

—BRUCE LYMBURN, PARTNER, WENDEL, ROSEN, BLACK & DEAN LLP

Clif Bar and Gary Erickson have waived the attorney-client privilege
to the extent necessary for Bruce Lymburn to tell this story.

gave him the same old story, "Clif Bar will never compete with the big guys. This is Gary's one shot. If he doesn't do this he will regret it the rest of his life." Hopefully he treated Bruce to lunch!

During negotiations the first question my partner's attorney asked me was, "Gary, why don't you just sell the company and begin a new venture?" My gut made me respond with one word, "No." I refused to consider that option. Since then I have witnessed many people start new companies after selling their first. It is rarely the same experience. I have traveled the globe and enjoyed numerous breathtakingly beautiful spots. But I have one favorite place in the world: A majestic canyon in the high Sierra complete with an alpine lake, rocky peaks, a creek, and luscious meadows. The question posed to me was like saying, "Why don't you find another perfect place?" I already knew my favorite place in the world. Clif Bar was my high Sierra canyon, my place in the world. I didn't want to look for another. It was time to return.

➤ BACK ON STAGE

No big "hooray" greeted me when I took back the company. Even though Clif Bar had only sixty-five employees, some people didn't even know who I was. I had essentially disappeared from the company as a means of coping with the tension between my former business partner and me during the period before the near sale. Morale was at an all-time low. People were exhausted from working hard to prepare the company for sale. Rumors flew. Some people were convinced that I would sell the company in three months, others that I would crack under the pressure. I worked four full-time jobs simultaneously during the early days of trying to rebuild the company:

- **MORALE OFFICER**: I didn't know if employees believed in Clif Bar Inc.—or in me—anymore. I didn't know if they could believe again.

- **OPERATIONS ER DOCTOR**: The year that I distanced myself from the company many operational issues developed that needed immediate attention: quality control, excess inventory, low profit, and general organization.

- **NEGOTIATOR**: My partnership unraveled. Within two weeks of the decision not to sell Clif Bar Inc. my partner and I had moved rapidly from mediation to communication through attorneys. Negotiations lasted seven months.

- **FUNDRAISER**: To buy my partner's half of the company I needed a lot of money. So, instead of walking away with $60 million in my pocket, I now had to finance a $62 million buyout plus financing costs.

I read a lot during those early stressful days. I remember being drawn to the story of Julia Butterfly Hill as told in her book *The Legacy of Luna*. When she was twenty-three years old, Julia climbed two hundred feet up a redwood tree to protest the logging of northern California's ancient redwood forests. She came down two years and eight days later after negotiating a deal with Pacific Lumber that preserved the tree and those surrounding it. She lived on a makeshift platform and endured winter storms, harassment, and loneliness. Ironically the name of her tree was Luna (I hope she ate some bars during her 738-day tree-sit!). Powerful forces rallied against this young

" I do not endorse products. I do, however, endorse beliefs and actions. A funny-sounding first sentence, one might think, but to me, this is core to who I am, and where I place the highest value.

I was raised to believe that a person's word is their bond. For me, this means that words must always be connected with actions. If the words are hollow, then so too is the value of the person saying them.

Clif Bar Inc. has only 'x' amount of value per unit price and as a company. But the commitment Gary has to protecting people, planet, and profit together as his 'triple bottom line' is priceless. It is these beliefs and value systems *in action* that inspire me.

We get misled into believing that economics is more important than anything else—that it is acceptable for people and the planet to be the ones to pay the high price for profit.

Yet if we look at the words *economics* and *ecologics,* we see they share the same root word *ecos,* which means 'house' or 'home.' Economics in its purest translation means, 'to take care of or steward one's home.' Our home is so much more than just a house. It is all life, interconnected and interdependent. We need to do a much better job of taking care of each other, our planet, and our children's future.

It is this deep-felt understanding that compelled me to live in a thousand-year-old redwood for more than two years in order to protect it and to call attention to the plight of our world's forests. I chose to sit in a tree as a commitment to a world that is healthy, just, and sustainable for all. Isn't it interesting to realize that an economy that will last for the long term must also invest in these same values. "

—JULIA BUTTERFLY HILL

woman. Big companies wanted to chop the tree down. Helicopters flew dangerously close to her. People harassed her. Yet she didn't climb out of the tree after the first storm, after the first threat; she stayed until the job was done. Julia inspired me. My "company-sit" might last indefinitely. Just as Julia had a handful of solid supporters, so did I. Kit never wavered in her belief in the company and in me. My family and close friends encouraged me and employees soon rallied again. But at times it felt incredibly lonely. Was it really possible to pull this off? Was I crazy to try?

➤ TURNING THE COMPANY AROUND

Certainly whether we were a "fit" company in a business sense was an issue. But Clif Bar Inc. had other problems. We had ignored in-house morale issues in our rush to put the company up for sale. I thought the company had become dysfunctional. With the letdown of not selling, the dysfunction grew.

When I walked back into Clif Bar I doubt anyone thought, "All right. Here comes Gary. He will save the day." One of the first things I did was to stand in front of the company and tell them how I felt and what I wanted to do. I knew at the time that my speech couldn't suddenly reassure Clif's employees. I knew it would take many conversations and an ongoing transparency to regain trust. I spent hours walking around the office talking with employees, getting to know people better, making myself a visible presence.

I needed to get company leaders, the people who managed and supervised employees, back on board as quickly as possible. I had to convince the leadership team that our drifting Clif Bar boat could get back on course—that we could plug the holes and stay afloat. Persuading people to believe we could make it was one of my hardest tasks. Some of the leaders were exhausted; others didn't belong at Clif Bar. One individual told me how tired he was, how he didn't know what to do. I said that I either wanted his resignation on my desk the following day, or his agreement to stick around and give me a couple of months. "But you have to believe," I said. "If things don't start to turn around in two months, I'll help you find another job. But you have to be completely here, not halfway. You need to believe we can turn the company around because you are a leader and people look to you. If you are ambivalent, the people who report to you are never going to make it." He stuck around. Others did too. Our turnaround showed me what could happen if people really believe.

Despite the near-sale and the morale plummet, Clif products were doing well on the market. Our consumers didn't know about the problems within the company. They loved our products. I knew that we just needed to start functioning as a team again to succeed. And we needed to commit. We needed to say, "We are going to do this. We will compete." The company needed a leader, and leaders, who believed that we could compete against the big guys.

When I took over I knew that I couldn't lead as if nothing needed fixing. For June 1, 2000, my journal reads, *"What's going to turn this company around?"* Below that question, I'd listed forty-three ideas. At the top of the list were my physical presence and my demonstrated commitment as CEO and owner. The following pages capture some of the essence of that list—changes I thought could get Clif Bar Inc. back on course.

Do We Have the Right People?

Now that it was my show I needed to take a close look at the actors, all the people who worked for the company. We had initiated a hiring freeze in the months prior to the sale. The problem was that during that same period we grew like crazy. Now we were short at least fifteen people and heavily dependent on temporary employees. We were running lean—too lean to grow a business and keep sane in the process. We had also placed an office expansion on hold, and people were working shoulder to shoulder in cramped spaces. In a sense, everything had been placed on hold until the company was sold. Why build new offices, why hire new people if the new company planned to take the company (but not its people) back to the Midwest?

I immediately lifted the hiring freeze, but we had to find the *right* people. Jim Collins writes in *Good to Great* that you must first *get the wrong people out and the right people in, then figure out where to go.* In the year after I took over managing daily operations we carefully recruited to keep the boat afloat. I also had to decide whether I wanted to keep the employees hired during the year and three months that my partner ran the company on her own. I faced the painful task of letting some employees go, including high-level management. Fortunately, many skilled and creative people had come to Clif Bar for the right reasons. They got it. They shared Clif's values. Clif employees believed in the product and knew that we were about more than making money. It didn't take long for Clif people to recover their passion.

Communication and Trust

My journal entry for June 1, 2000, read that we needed to cure the "disease of fear and anxiety" and the "disease of gossip." I initiated all-company meetings on Fridays, which morphed into Thursday Morning Meetings, which we still have today. Each week (with rare exceptions), the entire company meets in our new performing arts center (at the start we met in the gym). We begin with "Bagels and Donuts": fresh fruit, bagels, cream cheese, pastries, juices, coffee, tea, and a time for people to talk to each other casually. In the meeting that follows, I play David Letterman (and a bad one at that!). Sometimes I talk about the news as it relates to our business; sometimes I tell a story of a journey or adventure and compare it to our company's path. At times I interview employees or people from causes we support. Or we host a guest speaker such as Julia Butterfly Hill or Jeanne Rizzo of The Breast Cancer Fund. Sometimes we use a speakerphone to call an employee with congratulations on the birth of a baby, or we call a consumer who wrote us a nice letter. It's a time for company announcements live and in person. It's a time to cut loose and have fun, something we missed during the preceding years. We always end meetings by reading a consumer letter.

The Thursday Morning Meetings put me in front of the company; they allowed people to see my face and the faces of all those in leadership. In those first precarious months, it was difficult to stand in front of the company every week. I had to mean what I said. If I wasn't really committed, it would show. Having everybody together built trust. We could see clearly that we were one company. Regular all-company meetings helped to heal our "anxiety disorder" and cut into our "gossip disorder," although stopping gossip would take more and better communication.

I initiated book assignments, discussion groups, and volunteer activities to encourage interdepartmental friendships, cooperation, and communication. For example, when employees work with Habitat for Humanity, they work with twenty colleagues from five different departments to build a house. Camaraderie develops. One year we broke folks into interdepartmental groups of five to six people. Each group presented a chapter from a book on branding to another group. People in accounting had the opportunity to talk about branding rather than working on finance all day. This cross-fertilization made us more creative and discussions turned naturally to the values we wanted to maintain at Clif Bar.

I started having weekly lunches with departments and groups. I told managers "the walls must come down," and we began concentrated efforts at more direct communication company-wide. As managers began to believe again, they started communicating better with their own people. The Thursday Morning Meetings also helped bring down the walls. I asked managers, including myself, to get out of their seats and start walking around the office talking to people.

People want and need to see the leaders of a company, to talk with them. David Packard called this "management by walking around." I was interested in our people, and I discovered that my employees wanted me to be interested in them. It takes effort to remain transparent. We will never do this perfectly. At Clif Bar we work hard to create and re-create a culture characterized by honest, direct communication at all levels.

Processes and People

The year before we put the company up for sale we experienced our lowest profit margin since Clif's inception. Our revenue growth rate was 33 percent, which may sound high, but up to that point we had averaged 50–100 percent annually. The cost of our products skyrocketed during 1999 and early 2000, which directly affected our overall net profit. We experienced product quality issues. I also discovered that we carried too much inven-

" I'm a child psychiatrist. I love the ads which feature Cliff saying he worries too much about his son. I would love a poster of this ad so I could frame it and put it in my waiting room. Oh yeah, I'm a cyclist and triathlete and Clif Bars and Shots are all I ever eat. You rock. "

—CLIF CONSUMER

" Greetings from the High Sierra. We are a group of fun-loving, Clif Bar eating, forest-dwelling bird researchers. We eat on the fly and your energy bars are our only ways to get through these hard-core hours of birding. Thanks for caring about your customers and the environment. "

—CLIF CONSUMERS

" I cannot begin to explain how happy I am that you are bringing back the Mojo Bar and adding a couple of new flavors. Although I enjoy the whole line of Clif Bar products, not only because they taste so good, but also because of what your company stands for. I really admire your stand for environmental issues, your commitment to give back to the community. Sorry, I didn't mean to hop off the subject, I just wanted to say how happy I am that the MOJO is coming back, baby. I have been searching everywhere. I actually drove an hour when I heard that a store in Orange County had some. I bought every bar they had left! (3½ boxes!) Keep up the great job. Your customer for life. "

—CLIF CONSUMER

tory for a company that produces food products with a limited shelf life (eleven months). We carried so much inventory that we could stop producing several Luna flavors for a year and a half! Clif had outsourced its operations department in 1999. I decided to bring operations back in-house, and we got our inventory, quality issues, and profit margins back to health within months.

I sensed that departments, groups, even individuals, often worked in isolation. I noticed resentment between departments and between individuals. There were misgivings on the part of some individuals toward the company and its products. Someone actually told me they were suspicious of the ingredients we used because they had never seen the bakery. Secrecy was affecting morale. People wanted to see how the product they were selling was made. Although it was—and is—important to keep our intellectual property secure, we found ways to show people the essence of the baking process. During that first year on my own with the company, I took the entire staff on a tour of the bakery where Luna was made. The following year we threw a party at the Clif Bar bakery for our brokers and many staff. We structured ways for employees to see how other parts of the company (or its subcontractors) operated. I needed to find ways to build trust, both horizontally and vertically.

We needed to review our employee compensation package. What were people being paid? I worked hard with Human Resources on this initiative. First, we lifted the salary freeze that had been initiated while preparing the company for sale. We reviewed everyone's salaries. We changed our compensation packages, including base salary, annual incentive bonus, med-

ical and dental, 401(k), and all the rest. In many cases we
needed to adjust compensation upward to align ourselves with
market rates in the Bay Area. I wanted to make sure that we
were continuing to develop the best compensation packages
possible for a private company of our size.

Personal Learning

I had never run the company by myself. Now the buck stopped
with me, and I had a lot to learn. Even though I read slowly, I
studied books that I thought would help me. Today, books such
as *The Tipping Point, The Living Company, Good to Great, Saving the Corporate Soul, The Legacy of Luna,* and *The Dream
Society* line the shelves in my office. Back in 2000, I read voraciously to see how other companies thrived, especially private
companies. I learned from the experiences of private companies
that had gone public and then been sold, especially those I
greatly admired such as Ben & Jerry's and Odwalla. I sought
out other entrepreneurs for long conversations. I spent a weekend in Yosemite with Yvon and Malinda Chouinard of Patagonia. Yvon and Malinda share my vision for sustainable business
as well as my passion for the outdoors. On our climb and over
dinner I benefited from their wisdom. I met with Ben Cohen
from Ben and Jerry's. Other leaders in the food and beverage
industry, like Ken Grossman, owner of Sierra Nevada Brewery
(one of the largest privately held breweries in the nation)
inspired me. Lanny Vincent, an innovation and organizational
consultant who worked with us in 1998, became my key mentor.
I read as much as I could and sought out people who "felt right"
to talk to them about how other companies our size were dealing with growth, management, and leadership.

RAISING
THE
BAR

THE STORY OF CLIF BAR, INC.

> **CLIF JOY**

We don't take ourselves too seriously. We have fun and our advertising shows it. The creativity that we put forth shows that we know "it's only food" and are humble about it.

—CLIF BAR EMPLOYEE, OCTOBER 2001

Clif Bar had been a happy place to work. Now I sensed a lot of seriousness in people, which is good, but I also wanted to bring out our humor. I wanted the fun back. We found ways to recover Clif playfulness and humor. One year we held an "Iron Chef" contest. Sixteen three-person teams competed over the course of a year. Before each company meeting, two teams competed live, copying the television show *Iron Chef*. Everyone in the company tasted the entries and voted on the best recipe. The week's winners selected the food theme for the next competing groups. It was a blast. The whole company got into it and came up with creative names, wild costumes, and incredible recipes.

Doug came up with the idea for the Martini & Weenie party, now an annual (after work) event. The party features both ends of the food and drink spectrum: fancy martinis and hot dogs (all beef or soy), complete with relish, ketchup, and mustard. We play Frank Sinatra music and bubbles float through the air as Doug, David Jericoff (VP of human resources), and I blend mean martinis, cosmopolitans, or nonalcoholic concoctions (and of course we have designated drivers assigned). We invite vendors and friends and make T-shirts and caps for the party.

Somewhere along the way we had dropped our annual camping trips. We brought them back and now head to the Sierra every year to rock climb and mountain bike. We roast marshmallows over the campfire. We hang out. We also have an annual picnic in various places around the Bay Area. The annual Clif Bar ski trip is also a hit. People who have never skied before come on the trips and learn a new sport.

We have an "open dog" policy, so every day is "Bring Your Dog to Work Day"—that is, if you have a dog that is well trained (unlike mine). Scrubby (Chris in Information Technology's dog) became so popular that our CFO Stan Tanka made the official Scrubby Calendar. The calendar features Scrubby sporting a new costume each month. Stan sold the calendar to raise money for Meals on Wheels.

Clif Bar's spirit of humor, joy and adventure is back. We firmly believe that people need to recreate. There isn't any reason why you can't work hard, play hard, and have a sense of humor along the way.

RAISING
THE
BAR

THE STORY OF CLIF BAR, INC.

IRON CHEF CONTEST.
—PAUL MCKENZIE

IRON CHEF TEAMS

Two Masters and a Mixer, Team Kaga-san, **Godlike Gourmets**, 2 Sisters & a Brother, Butter, **Cirque de Saute**, Shoo Fly Pie, 2 Steves & a Yana, The 3 Chef Rigos, The Saucy Saute-ers, Oval Team, Cast Iron Chefs, LTD, Team Scrubby, Fud Manchew, Exoticos al Minuto, Fresh Moho, Cooking Peoples, 2 Meats & a Veggie, Swordfish Trombone

➤ CLIF'S MOJO

To me mojo means, "You got that engine running baby and the
sky is the limit!" Clif Bar is the house that mojo built.

—CLIF BAR EMPLOYEE, OCTOBER 2001

Even during the first tough months our products did really well.
This gave us time to obtain financing, work through the partnership dissolution, and get the company going again. We were
growing dramatically, yet we had operational issues. And I was
on a soul-searching journey—for the essence of Clif Bar. I
wanted to know what kind of company we could become. I still
wondered if we would eventually need to find an equity partner.
People challenged me, including work colleagues, about whether
we could remain private. One employee told me, "It's just a matter of time, because when the check is big enough, you will sell."
I remained committed to keeping the company private.

"What kind of company do we want to be?" was the question I
kept asking myself. In fall 2000, Al Springer introduced himself
at the Natural Products Expo East. Al had made a name for
himself at Gatorade (owned by Quaker Oats), Dole Food Company, and other companies for his marketing savvy. Al was intrigued by our decision to stay private. After watching our booth
he said to me, "There is something going on at your booth.

There is a buzz. Look over there at [that competitor's] booth. It's dead." Then he said something that set my head spinning, something that became a watchword for me. He said, "They lost their mojo."

I realized Clif Bar had something—call it *mojo* or whatever word works for you. There was something about the brand, product, and way of being in the world that was different. I realized that mojo was an elusive quality and needed to be carefully tended. Companies lost it in different ways. Selling your company could be one way of losing it. It might not be obvious to consumers at first, but I believed that at some point consumers would respond negatively to companies that had it and lost it (whatever "it" was).

I returned to the office and told the story at an all-company meeting. I said, "I would like you guys to help me out. I'm giving you a homework assignment. I know that everybody has a lot of work to do, but I want you to take on this extra task." The first assignment: "Pick a company that had mojo and lost it. Why did they have it? How did they lose it?" Dozens of people turned in homework full of insightful responses. The following are samples from the "How Did They Lose Their Mojo?" homework assignment. (I leave company names out.)

- They failed to retain the culture as they grew in size, losing their creative juices.

- They ignored the value of their employees and moved the company headquarters from California to Colorado because the new CEO wanted to live there. This resulted in low morale and dysfunction.

- They forgot about the emotional connection with the consumer (and why they got into the business in the first place) and concentrated on the process of business. When someone spends $1.50 on an energy bar, they're buying a piece of their identity and not just convenient snack food. These people want to associate themselves with companies, products, brands that they feel good about.

- The company moved from being perceived as authentic and moved toward commercialism and money-monsterism. They lack Authenticity, Quality, and Social Integrity.

- I think the trick is to get bigger but not before you get better. You gotta maintain the edge and be a little bold. You gotta remember the roots, thank the little people, think about those that are less fortunate, support those that have been loyal . . . and then move on to the new kids in town. Getting big is risky and compromises the mojo if one is not careful. But it can be done.

Themes emerged. Companies lost their mojo for a combination of the following reasons: focus on cost reduction, decreased quality of the product, losing their own identity and uniqueness by mimicking others, straying from simple concepts, losing touch with the consumer, moving away from organizational strengths, trying too hard for the mass market, jumping on the bandwagon, losing innovation, becoming "greedy," decreasing customer service, thinking more of the business than of the consumer, not paying attention to community relations, losing authenticity, and losing an open, innovative, creative culture.

I learned from my employees. I integrated their insights into my vision for business. They believed in companies that paid attention to quality over cost reduction. They thought companies should "keep it simple" and stick to what they did best. Authenticity, creativity, innovation, and close ties to the community and consumer were high on their lists.

I wanted Clif Bar's mojo strong and growing. On October 1, 2001, I gave another homework assignment to the entire company. The Mojo Homework for 2001 consisted of these questions:

Does Clif Bar Inc. have mojo?

If so, why does Clif Bar have it?

In what ways is Clif Bar teetering and risking losing it?

What things could really cause us to lose it?

How can we get more of it?

In what ways can you personally affect our mojo, both positively and negatively?

The response to this and later homework amazed me. People took the assignments seriously. Their answers spoke to our company's core values, our reasons for being, our passion and integrity. We bound the answers in notebooks and displayed twelve copies prominently in the main office so that anyone could read the Mojo Homework (they are still there). I include a few examples of the Clif Mojo Homework here:

- If you asked me this question last year, I would say we had practically lost our mojo. Because of the uncertainty of our future last year with the possible sale of the company, many felt that the passion was dead. Many felt that it really is a big dog eat little dog world. By not believing in ourselves to compete against the big dogs, we will be eaten alive.

- We are known as the cool company. We are looked at as the company that sticks to its values, no matter what. We support the communities that we sell in. We don't cut corners on our ingredients.

- The best way to get more mojo is by not forcing it. Doing it artificially can really damage us.

- I firmly believe that Clif Bar has mojo not because of the products, but because of the people behind the products. Yes, we have great-tasting-kick-the-competition's-butt bars, but that's only part of the story. The people at Clif Bar are genuinely good people. We also truly believe in our products, each other—do you know how rare that is?

- We could easily lose our mojo if we fall into the traps of cost cutting and compromising quality and losing our identity of being a positive force in people's lives—it is not all about profits.

- Clif Bar may teeter on losing its mojo if being the most profitable becomes its sole goal. One of Clif Bar's challenges, as we grow larger and more profitable, will be remaining focused on the original vision.

- Should Clif Bar become too comfortable, we could lose the mojo. Without a continued drive to take risks and find new, innovative and exciting ways to make our products better and the company stronger.

- If we grow too fast too soon we can lose it. If we decided to go public or sell the company that would be the end.

- I do have a (small) fear that we will get so big that we forget where we came from. That we'll forget to dance with the one who brought us.

- I think if Clif Bar Inc. loses its values/qualities it could lose its mojo. We should not follow the typical American Dream— "Own your business, and grow it as quickly as you can until you can cash out. . . ." I am convinced that Clif Bar Inc. really lost its mojo in 1999.

RAISING THE BAR

THE STORY OF CLIF BAR, INC.

RAISING

THE BAR

THE STORY OF CLIF BAR, INC.

" Mojo is power and magic and goodness—it's an intangible thing that can't be adequately described in words. It's a good feeling. It's people you love, a summer day in Maui—a Clif Bar in your backpack to share with the guy who stops to talk and find out who you are instead of walking by without making eye contact. It's the right thing to do. We can't sell out—it's simply not worth it in a world where it sometimes seems like nobody cares and if you call a customer service line you get a computer with a zillion lines and no Real People. We are Real People. Clifford Answers Our Phones. We Listen. We Really Care About Our Products. We Really Care About Our World. There's nothing wrong with making money—we all need it to live. Money used wisely is another form of good energy. I'm proud that Clif is giving the world a healthy alternative in energy food and especially proud that we're doing it the way we are. CLIF = MOJO. "

—LESLIE HENRICHSEN, GARY AND KIT'S ASSISTANT

- We need to maintain our customer-friendly approach. Even as we see the need to grow, we need to stay down to earth and a little offbeat.

The homework assignments gave me a clearer understanding of how employees felt about Clif Bar. They gave people a way to express what Clif Bar could be, and the assignments helped guide our vision for the future. Clif Bar will always be a work in progress, yet our clarity today is light years ahead of 1999 and early 2000.

➤ MOVING TO SUSTAINABILITY—
REDUCING OUR ECOLOGICAL FOOTPRINT

I realized that my concern for the environment was missing from my present life. Clif had elements of environmental awareness but no concerted, committed effort. I turned to Elysa Hammond. Elysa was my wife's best friend growing up. She and I met at California Polytechnic University in San Luis Obispo. She majored in agriculture and I in business. She was an A student and I . . . well, a solid C+ student. (I still try to hire people smarter than I am!) We became great friends, and she taught me about the environment, about agriculture, about world hunger. I watched her conduct research all over the world as her career unfolded. From Mexico to Borneo, Elysa pursued her

RAISING THE BAR

THE STORY OF CLIF BAR, INC.

passion for sustainable agriculture. Now she was living in New York and had three small children. I called her.

During our telephone conversation I asked Elysa to work for Clif as our in-house ecologist. At the time of that first conversation, I didn't know enough to use the term SUSTAINABILITY. I thought that ORGANIC about covered what we wanted to do as a company. But Elysa said to me, "You know, I think that we are talking about more than organic; we are talking about SUSTAINABILITY." My learning curve was steep as I attempted to answer certain questions: What was sustainability? How did it apply to Clif Bar Inc.? (Chapter Seven outlines my business model for sustainability.) Elysa continues to be our in-house ecologist and helps the company (and me) understand what we can do to reduce our ecological footprint on the planet.

In 2000 we initiated the Clif Bar Environmental Program. By 2003 all Clif Bar flavors were certified organic, making us the largest organic energy and nutrition bar company on the market. Employees voluntarily conducted "environmental audits" on all aspects of Clif Bar operations. We found ways to use organic cotton in all our T-shirts, recycled paper in our publications, and to cut our energy usage company-wide. Clif's move toward sustainability galvanized the company as much as any other initiative. Moving toward sustainability inspired and motivated people.

I learned that people get excited about creating concrete ways to express their values. The entire company shared the desire to reduce Clif's ecological footprint. The Clif Bar Environmental Program was another key move that helped turn the business around and added depth to our vision.

> LIVING IN THE GRAY— CREATING A CULTURE OF QUESTIONING

I knew we could turn Clif Bar around; I didn't know how exactly. We were living in the gray area, and the uncertainty made a lot of people uncomfortable. They wanted black-and-white answers. They wanted to know if we could compete, if we could fund our growth. I didn't have the answers. In fact, I believed that in the long run having questions was more important than having answers. I wanted to create a culture of questioning. The homework assignments helped. Instead of beginning with certainties, we began by asking good questions. One Friday morning I told the company, "Don't be afraid to ask those questions, the ones you don't have an answer for." In small group meetings, people got thrown off when others made

RAISING THE BAR

THE STORY OF CLIF BAR, INC.

absolute statements, so I coached people on how to ask questions rather than stake out turf. Questions turned into new homework assignments that helped us analyze Clif. People asked: "Can we have heart? Can we keep a company with heart?" I created homework based on those questions. I told people to find a company that had heart and analyze why. "Find a brand. Bring it to work." At the Friday meeting when the assignment was due, boxes of product surrounded us, and people explained why they thought certain brands had heart. Getting comfortable with uncertainty and learning how to ask questions boosted company morale. Employees began to face challenges with excitement instead of dread.

Anxiety and fear decrease when we become comfortable living in the gray area. The whole mood of a group or company can change when people are not expected to have all the answers. Some people will be uncomfortable in the gray zone. We grow up learning that everything is black and white. Yes, some things may be black and white, but for Clif Bar and me, gray areas exist, places where answers and choices are not clear. Creating a culture of questioning and exploring is key for any entrepreneur.

> ### ➤ SWIMMING WITH THE BIG FISH

One question dominated leading up to and following the near-sale of the company: Can we compete? Essentially, we had two brands driving the growth of the company. We knew we were competing against the big guys, and we were competing without the traditional external funding that conventional wisdom claims is crucial. Although most experts said we couldn't compete, that never made sense to me. Before Clif Bar existed, back when Doug and I were developing the package, he asked me, "So, how big do you think this could be?" I replied, "Man, if we could break a million dollars in sales that would be something." We had grown, dramatically, and were continuing to grow. I looked around and saw other small companies that continued to grow. We weren't going backward. Yet everyone said we couldn't swim with the big fish.

I got to know and respect Bob Gamgort, the president of the North America division of Mars, in 1999 when they wanted to invest in our company. (Mars never bid for Clif Bar when we were up for sale.) After we took the company off the market, Bob called me. I told him how important it was for me to keep the company private, and Bob respected my decision. A week later he sent me the book *Eating the Big Fish* by Adam Morgan with a card that read, "Congratulations on your decision. Good luck and I hope the best for you. You have a great company. I know you can do it. I know you can make it." Bob was virtually the only "expert" telling me we could compete. I read *Eating the Big Fish*. It described how small companies could compete around the big fish—the large companies.

How did we compete as a small fish? First, we convinced Clif people to believe that we could compete. Second, we made sure that our products remained the best on the market, with the highest-quality ingredients. We followed natural demand; Luna was a good example. With virtually no advertising, Luna entered the market and did $10 million in sales in its first year, followed by $29 million the following year. We had cool packaging. We told a great (and true) company story. Our consumers didn't know the struggles we went through to remain private. Yet anyone who read the back of the package or tasted the bar understood that a lot of care went into the product. We pulled off what you might call the Cinderella Story.

➤ WE'RE BACK

Within two years of nearly selling the company we refinanced our entire debt, buying back all the remaining stock. How did this happen? In December 2001, Kit—knowing that I encouraged a culture of questioning—asked me some simple questions about our debt. "How much do we owe now, and how much will we owe at the end of the five-year period? Is there any way we could just own the company now? Can't we pay a bank instead of Lisa?" I went to our CFO, Stan Tanka, with Kit's questions and found out that now was the time. Stan, and the team he assembled, created a magical package—or "management presentation," as they say in the funding business. We shopped around and found banks willing to work with us. We hired SPP Capital Partners, LLC, a boutique investment-banking firm, to broker the deal. We bought out the remaining partnership debt with a loan from Union Bank of California and a subordinate note from Allied Capital, saving us nearly $8 million in interest. *Best of all: On August 2, 2002, Kit and I became 100 percent owners of Clif Bar Inc.* We went from 50 percent to 67 percent to 100 percent ownership within two years. I gave personalized medallions to everyone in the company, thanking them for their contribution to Cinderella Story number two. My business partner received her final payment, marking the last chapter in her connection to the company.

Back in 2000, we were told that we couldn't compete, that we would be marginalized, that we would be bought off the shelf within six months. Instead, we grew from $40 million to over $100 million in annual sales in under three years. We did this without external funding, while burdened with incredible debt. Luna and Clif Bar were the number one bars in natural foods, bike, and outdoor channels with a 35 percent market share. Luna ranked #1 and Clif Bar #3 in grocery. Luna Bar overtook PowerBar as the #1 bar in the country in grocery, natural, and outdoor channels. Yet much more important than annual sales was the fact that *we* were back as a living, thriving company. My personal life changed as well: I started riding my bike again, I slept better, I regained my sense of humor, and my family life improved. Not only was Clif back, *I* was back.

We've got our mojo back. We keep asking great questions. We have wonderful, motivated people. We continue to make healthy, tasty products. With vision and belief you can surmount incredible odds.

> **EPIPHANY REVISITED**

Ten years after my 175-mile "epiphany" ride with Jay, I stood in front of the company and told the story of the journey that began it all. Some had heard part of the story before, but to most people it was new. I told the company I wanted to ride again. This time with them. I told them, "If I didn't ride that day. If I didn't ride that distance and eat all those bars, you wouldn't be sitting here right now. I want to celebrate that. I want to celebrate the birth of an idea and what that idea has become."

In November 2000 Clif Bar Inc. initiated the first Annual Epiphany Ride. We rode the same route. Not everyone could ride all 175 miles so we added 100- and 35-mile options. Twelve people completed the 175-mile ride, two joined us for the 100-mile option, and fifty-odd met us for the last 35 miles, including Kit, members of the U.S. Postal Service Pro Cycling Team, friends of the company, and lots of employees.

The original epiphany happened because I was tired of an energy bar. Now I wanted to prove I could eat a lot of Clif Bar products without becoming sick of them. So, as an addition to the event, for the seven days before the ride I ate nothing but Clif Bars, Luna Bars, and Clif Shot. The company watched me carefully. People tried to help me by concocting recipes with Clif products. (Thanks, Chelseah and Blue!) People cut and toasted bars. Janet actually baked a pie using one product for the crust and Clif Shot for filling. By the end of the week I had eaten forty-five Clif Bars, twenty Luna Bars, and forty-two Clif Shots. I wasn't just testing if I would tire of the products; I also wanted to know how I would perform on a 175-mile bike ride after eating only our products for a week. Fellow cyclists challenged me on the ride. A film crew made a documentary of the journey. As it turns out, I had one of my best cycling days in years. It was a blast!

The first Annual Epiphany Ride felt like a rallying point for the company. It had been seven months since we took the

**CLIF ANNUAL
EPIPHANY RIDE.**
—LESLIE HENRICHSEN

RAISING
THE BAR

THE STORY OF CLIF BAR, INC.

CLIF GROUPIES (DEBBIE AND LESLIE)
—STEPHEN HOUGHTON

MOM, DAD, AND FAMILY AT FIRST
ANNUAL EPIPHANY RIDE.
—DIANE CRAWFORD

company off the market. We were celebrating the beginnings of our unique company. Morale was good. I believe people felt that they were a living part of the vision. Every year since then more people have joined the Annual Epiphany Ride, including people who had never ridden a bike in their lives. People prepare months ahead of time in special programs designed by Clif trainers.

Epiphany ride number one—1990. No company, no money, no bar, nothing. Just one idea. Now our company celebrates the idea (and reality) annually. The Epiphany Ride symbolizes that we are back and it remains one of the best company events of the year. It is not just a great party. It is an event in which everyone feels that they have accomplished something and that they are part of the vision.

On the first Annual Epiphany Ride Celebration in 2000, Kit and I were among the last to return. At the end of the ride stood my parents, Cliff and Mary, holding a large sign reading "Clif 4 Ever."

We were back.

RAISING
THE
BAR

THE STORY OF CLIF BAR, INC.

CHAPTER 4 **WHITE ROAD/RED ROAD**

(A PHILOSOPHY FOR LIFE AND BUSINESS)

In 1986 I asked my friend Jay to cycle the Alps with me. "Meet me in
Lucerne," I said. I wanted us to ride our bikes over the major
European passes that we'd heard about from the Tour de
France, Tour of Switzerland, and Giro di Italia. We'd already
climbed some of the peaks. Now I wanted us to experience
cycling up and down these passes on a thousand-mile-plus tour
while gazing at some of the world's most beautiful mountains.
Although I had never done a trip this ambitious before, I told
Jay, "I have a map. I've been to Europe; you've been to Europe.
Let's go." We wanted to travel light, so instead of loading ourselves down with fifty to eighty pounds of gear we carried
packs that weighed about eight pounds. We strapped our
mini-packs (the size of shoeboxes) under our bike seats.

On that first trip, as on the twenty others that followed,
everything that needed doing, we did. We fixed our own bikes
and cleaned our clothes every night. We planned the route,
exchanged money, found food and hotels—even after riding a

"Meet me in Lucerne, Switzerland."

hundred miles over three or four mountain passes. We rode in rain and snow. Steep grades punished us; downhills (which could last up to an hour) exhilarated us. We got lost, hungry, dehydrated, and hypothermic, and sometimes we drank too much beer. Our rewards for struggling over intense switchback roads on high passes were the spectacular vistas of snowy mountains, deep verdant valleys, alpine lakes, and storybook villages. Little did I know that this trip, and those that followed, would provide the foundation for my life and business philosophy.

➤ THE RIGHT MAPS

We left Lucerne early in the morning that first day and headed for a big alpine pass. We knew the route we needed—a road to the Grosse Scheidegg. We studied the map and saw one road, colored red, heading straight for our pass. That was our road! We headed out on the road marked red, barely able to contain our excitement. Yet excitement quickly turned to dismay as cars and trucks whizzed by us on the freeway. A motorist pulled us over and yelled at us in English, "Bicycles are not allowed on this road. It is illegal." Feeling like dumb Americans we left the highway and asked people for alternate routes to the pass. We found less busy roads through the countryside and made it to our first night's destination. We gazed at spectacular mountains, some that we had climbed and others we hoped to climb in the future. We figured we'd just made a mistake earlier. It didn't occur to us that maybe we had the wrong map.

On our second day we barely noticed the majesty of the Eiger because a brutal rainstorm overtook us as we rode over a

MICHAEL IN FRONT OF THE EIGER (1987)

nine-thousand-foot mountain pass. In spite of a close encounter with hypothermia we made it to our destination. Over the next days we traversed major European mountain passes and cycled through lovely villages. Each evening we sampled delicious regional food. We rode through the gorgeous wine country surrounding Montreaux (home to a famous jazz festival) and headed on to Chamonix, a mecca for mountain climbing and skiing.

In Chamonix we started to figure out that we had the wrong map. Our map covered large areas of Italy, France, Germany, and Switzerland. It was true that our trip snaked through parts of these areas, but as we cycled we noticed lots of small roads that weren't marked on our map. Where did these roads lead? The following day we bought a map with more detail to plan the route to our next destination—the town of Bourg-St. Maurice. Looking at the new map we realized, "There are fifty choices here. We don't have to go on those busy roads." We began searching out small roads and alternative passes. That day we climbed four passes, some barely wide enough for one car, and ended up in Bourg-St. Maurice. I can't begin to describe our excitement at finding these roads.

After Chamonix we got serious about our maps and routes, and as we pored over maps, the nature of our trip changed. It stopped being about traveling from Point A to Point B. It turned into a true adventure. By following tiny country roads we avoided the well-traveled areas and courted surprises. Exploring cool new roads and discovering routes that had never been traveled by bicycle came to define our journey.

We learned the importance of getting the right map.

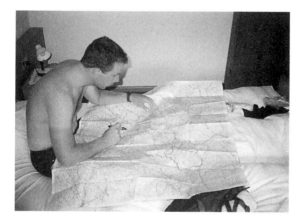

JAY STUDIES THE MAP

RAISING THE BAR

THE STORY OF CLIF BAR, INC.

The next day we wanted to lunch in Courmayeur (a famous climbing village in Italy). That night we studied our maps and found a pass that would take us from Courmayeur back to Switzerland via the Col Ferret. The route seemed particularly interesting because it looked as if no road existed at the top of the pass, possibly just a trail or dirt road. From Bourg-St. Maurice we ascended the Petit St. Bernard and crossed into Italy for the first time on our trip. We splurged on an incredible Italian meal, spending more than our meager budget allowed. Fortified by pasta, dessert, bread, and too much wine, we headed straight into Mont Blanc and headed for Col Ferret, the only place where France, Italy, and Switzerland meet. As we suspected, the paved road eventually ended and turned into a steep and grueling dirt path. It's important to remember that we were riding road bikes, not mountain bikes. At times we carried our bikes over our shoulders. It took us a long time. We didn't reach the top of the pass until near dark and had no idea how long it would take us to descend. We rode down the mountain on a single-track trail. Mammoth glaciers and alpine meadows slipped into shadow as we passed. It was pitch black by the time we reached pavement, and we were still miles from the nearest village. Riding slowly we finally arrived at a chalet, where we gratefully consumed large quantities of wiener

"Mammoth glaciers
and alpine meadows
slipped into the shadow
as we passed."

COL FERRET (ITALY)

schnitzel and beer, reflecting on another incredible day in the Alps and our good fortune in discovering back roads.

The picture on the cover of this book is from the trail to Col Ferret. We loved the difficult dirt track route we chose. We loved adventure. Together, Jay and I had scaled big walls in Yosemite Valley, climbed Mount Rainer, and slept on ten-inch-wide ledges while roped into granite rock faces. Our Col Ferret day brought together a lot of what we loved: We were high in the mountains where we felt comfortable; we were cycling; and we were nearly climbing since we'd had to hike over a snowfield that day (while carrying our bicycles!). Plus, at the end of this and every day on the trip, we ate great food, stayed in beautiful alpine villages, and met wonderful people. We were living a great adventure.

➤ FINDING THE WHITE ROADS

Our trip kept getting better and better now that we knew the types of roads we wanted to travel. The map made it very clear which roads would be busy with lots of buses, trucks, and cars, and which would be quiet, narrow, country roads. The Michelin maps defined roads as red, yellow, or white. Main roads, busy with buses, trucks, and cars, were marked boldly in red. Yellow roads were minor arteries, not as big as red roads but well traveled. The hundreds of roads branching off from the red and yellow roads were marked in white. We started on the red road, moved to the yellow, and by day three our mantra became *ride the white road.* White roads held adventure as well as the most spectacular views. We met people face-to-face rather than at tour bus stops or gas stations. On our Col Ferret day we pushed the white-road journey to another level. We connected a white road with another white road by dirt trail, even though it had meant walking with our bikes on our backs.

As we continued on our white-road journey, we climbed famous passes like the Passo Gavia, the Stelvio, the Furka, and the Splügen. We climbed ten thousand feet and cycled at least eighty miles every day. We pedaled more than twelve hundred miles during our fourteen-day trip. We felt happy with our performance and exhilarated by the adventure, the people we met, and the beauty of the roads. We hadn't started out with a final destination in mind, and when our time was up, we found ourselves in Innsbruck, Austria. I returned to northern Italy to design bicycle seats and Jay finally threw away the socks he had worn (and never washed) for fourteen days and left to climb the Eiger with world-famous mountain climber Mugs Stump. We were as strong as we had ever been and as happy. We relished the white roads, the true roads "less traveled."

RAISING THE BAR

THE STORY OF CLIF BAR, INC.

"The white road
is quiet. It's about simplicity."

I learned a lot on this trip. White-road and red-road journeys are qualitatively different. You need the right map. On the red road it is about the destination. On the white road it is about the road. On the white road you must travel light. The white road is quiet. It's about simplicity. It's often adventurous. You need to dig deep. Sometimes there is no road. You have to trust your gut.

Years later I began to see the relationship between this journey and our business. Not many people have done a trip like our white-road adventure. Not many companies would decide to do a journey like our white-road epic. I believe companies choose their roads—white, yellow, or red. Clif Bar strives to be on the white-road journey (but that hasn't always been the case).

➤ IT'S ABOUT THE DESTINATION:
A COMPANY ON THE RED ROAD

Red marks the widest, fastest road, the most direct and quick route between Point A and Point B. *On the red road it's about the destination.* The largest red roads are freeways; often bicycles are not allowed, as we discovered. Even if bicycles are allowed, you will encounter heavy car, truck, and bus traffic.

When you pull your bike over at a hotel or café you encounter tourists, not locals; fast food, not regional cuisine. On the red road a truck may make an innocent mistake and swerve into your path. The red road is dangerous, noisy, hackneyed, stressful, and full of risk that is out of your control.

Paradoxically, certain types of risk are minimized on the red road. You can always find a gas station, hotel, or store if you need food or assistance. You can stick out your thumb for a ride to the next town. You always find people. Sometimes you may get on a red road without realizing it, and at times the red road may be the only way to get from Point A to Point B.

A company on the red road believes business is about the destination; about moving from Point A to Point B. A red-road company's primary reason for being, its destination, is maximizing shareholder value; the essence of maximizing shareholder value is financial gain. When shareholder value and the bottom line become *the* reasons for being in business, everything else feeds that agenda. You might call an energy bar company with this red-road agenda *Bottom Line Bar Inc.* From 1998 to April 2000, I fell into a way of thinking that I had avoided previously and found myself the co-owner of *Bottom Line Bar.* Somehow making money and "growing" Clif Bar turned into our primary

BOTTOM LINE BAR INC.

reason for being. We still cared about our employees and making a great product, but they took second seat. In 1998 fourteen Clif managers met together for a two-day retreat to develop "Big Hairy Audacious Goals" for the company. Twelve of the seventeen goals we developed were about money, the bottom line on the red road. In 1999 I was part of a small upper-management group that created a strategy document based on red-road principles. The plan's goals required external funding. Following this strategic plan led us to almost sell the company in April 2000.

> **THE FUN OF GETTING THERE
IS GETTING THERE: A COMPANY
ON THE WHITE ROAD**

On the white road, the moment—the journey itself—matters
most. When you're riding a mountain bike down a difficult section of trail you worry about where you are *at that moment*. If
you think about your destination, if you take your focus off the
path beneath you, falling becomes inevitable. White-road companies don't have a set or final destination: The trip could end
anywhere. What would a final destination for Clif Bar Inc. be?
Would it be selling the company? Reaching a certain monetary
goal? Employing a certain number of people? Boasting two
hundred different products? Those aren't our ultimate goals.
We plan like any company does, but we center our discussion
on what roads we'd like to travel and the type of business we'd
like to become. *The road, not the destination, drives Clif Bar.*

Kit and I decided to stay owners of the company and run the
risks that come with riding the white road. Risks on the white
road come from the road itself. Maybe the road is unimproved
or banked by cliffs that you could plunge over riding too fast on
a downhill stretch. You could ride along huge, steep rock faces
prone to rockslides. Or you could get caught in bad weather

while high in the mountains and far from shelter, as Jay and I did. On the red road there's one primary risk: getting hit by a car or truck over which you have no control. For a public company, getting hit by a truck might translate into being acquired by a larger company. In other words—you are affected by someone else's actions.

Traveling the white road places risk in your own hands, not in the hands of others.

We have some maps and create new ones as we go, but we have no guidebook. *Bottom Line Bar* had one reason for being—maximizing shareholder value through growth and making money. The white-road journey shaped my philosophy of life and underlies how I run a business. Clif Bar has been guided by the principles of the white-road journey described in this chapter.

Our white-road company has not one but five reasons for being: sustaining our brands, our company, our people, our community, and our planet. These five elements form an interconnected system, the Clif Bar ecosystem (described in Chapter Seven). We take great care with each part of the Clif ecosystem. Sustaining our people, one of the aspirations, is not a means to an end (profit or maximizing shareholder value), but a value in and of itself. If Clif Bar attempted to grow at a rate of 200–250 percent over the next three years we'd need to hire a hundred people and work the entire staff extraordinarily hard. To double Clif Bar in three years, we would have to borrow money or take on new equity partners. To a red-road way of thinking, this is a reasonable business strategy, but here at Clif we aim to sustain our employees. Demanding seventy to eighty hours a week means that employees would exercise less, have less free time to re-create themselves, and less time with their families: Their lives and health would become out of balance. If we worked our employees that hard they would have to stop giving hours to nonprofit organizations, thus negatively affecting our community service program. If we hired and attempted to integrate a lot of new employees quickly, we'd run the risk of damaging our corporate culture. In other words, we'd end up leaving the white for the more-traveled red road.

THE WHITE ROAD: IT'S ABOUT THE JOURNEY

You must take a leap of faith

You must listen to your gut

You must travel light

Detailed map required

It's about simplicity—**eat, sleep, ride**

You desire to find new roads—sometimes there is no road

Hundreds of choices

Risk is in your hands

It's fun

You must be sensitive to local culture

You must be creative

You must be open to change

Sense of humor needed

It's Quiet

You must be honest

You must trust your fellow riders

It's often adventurous

There is freedom

(CHECKING THE MAP) **ONE MORE TIME**

RAISING THE BAR

THE STORY OF CLIF BAR, INC.

RAISING THE BAR

THE STORY OF CLIF BAR, INC.

THE RED ROAD: IT'S ABOUT THE DESTINATION

No need to take a leap of faith

No need to trust your gut

No need to travel light

One un-detailed map required

It's busy

No need to find cool new roads

Few choices

Someone else controls risk

It's boring

No need to be sensitive to the culture

No need to be creative

No need to be open to change

No need to have a sense of humor

Loud and noisy—distorts clear thinking

No need to be honest

No need to trust others

No need to desire adventure

Your route is predetermined

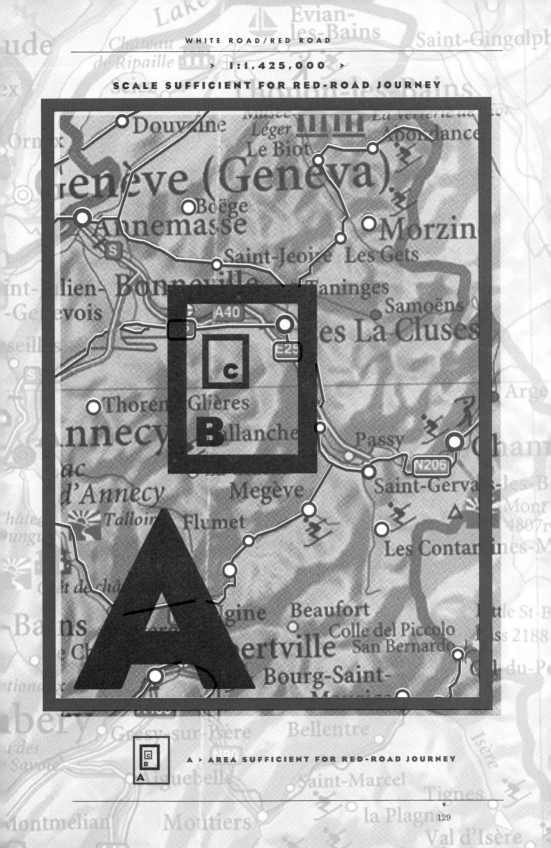

A > AREA SUFFICIENT FOR RED-ROAD JOURNEY

> 1:100,000 >

SCALE NEEDED FOR WHITE-ROAD JOURNEY

C

B

B > AREA NEEDED FOR WHITE-ROAD JOURNEY

130

> 1:100,000 (DETAIL) >

SCALE NEEDED FOR WHITE-ROAD JOURNEY

C > DETAIL OF AREA NEEDED FOR WHITE-ROAD JOURNEY

➤ THE RIGHT MAPS REVISITED

If the main goal of a business is to get from Point A to Point B, to grow revenues as quickly as possible, a detailed map isn't necessary. You can follow a fairly straightforward red-road formula: use the cheapest ingredients or parts for your product; forecast exactly how a new product will perform in your presentation to the board or shareholders; dump a lot of money into launching a new product; crank out the revenue. These tried-and-true formulas don't work on the white road. To travel the white road, you need a map that shows all the small roads and the entire topography. It has to be detailed because white-road businesses use maps to explore alternative routes. They look for the wild little roads. Few companies risk following routes that may not get you over the pass. Most want the certainty of success. Our attitude is, "Let's plant it and see how the market reacts." Launching the Luna Bar is a wonderful example. We thought we might reach $1.5 million in sales if all went well. We studied the map carefully but had no idea we would reach $10 million in sales the first year. Making a bar targeted for women was a road no one had taken. In fact, as I mentioned in Chapter Two, big companies and industry experts criticized us for limiting it to women. The red road is densely populated; why ride out on a wild road that may cut off half your market?

If the Luna story shows how taking a white road can open new territory, Rapid Quench shows how it can lead to a dead end. We created Clif Bar as an alternative to PowerBar. Using that model we introduced an alternative to Gatorade in 1994: Rapid Quench sports drink. We created Rapid Quench from real fruit juice as an alternative to drinks on the market made of sugar and fructose. We figured that if we could grab even a share point of Gatorade's billion-dollar market we would be doing very well indeed. It seemed like a natural move for us. In this case our white-road decision didn't pan out. Instead we found that liquid is heavy, making shipping expensive. The distribution and sales organization differed dramatically from what we were used to, as did the margins. White roads don't always pan out; we explored this road and found a dead end. Since we were traveling light we didn't spend much money on launching the product and it didn't hurt us too badly.

RAISING
THE
BAR

THE STORY OF CLIF BAR, INC.

> **SIMPLICITY**

Eat. Sleep. Ride.

Eat. Sleep. Ride.
Eat. **Sleep.** Ride.

Eat.
Sleep.
Ride.
Eat. Sleep. Ride.

Eat.

Sleep.
Ride.
Eat. Sleep. **Ride.** Get the point?

Jay and I stripped our lives
down to the basics on
our white-road journey.
Simplicity became the
trip's theme.

EAT > SLEEP > RIDE

And what a simple, wonderful, full life it was. On our trip we had everything we needed. We rode our bikes eight to twelve hours a day. We feasted on Europe's best regional food. We stayed in cool, quirky pensiones, chalets, and hotels every night.

I find simplicity also works in business. Private ownership is simple. Growing at a natural and controlled rate is simple. Not needing to search for outside money is simple. Creating natural products that taste good is simple. Life was simple in the early days at Clif Bar, when we had few employees and products, and it's certainly true that every person or product we add makes our business more complex. At our core, though, we maintain simple values that don't change as we add people, products, and profits. Our products feature simple, natural ingredients that are as close to the original sources as possible. Our organizational structure remains relatively simple, with fewer hierarchical layers than is the norm in business. Decision making and direct communication happen relatively quickly; they don't bog down traveling through a corporate maze—owner, board of directors, multiple shareholders, managers, middle managers, and so on. In our advertising, we tell stories. We hope that by telling stories we communicate simple messages that involve our consumers in deciding about buying a product, rather than manipulating them to buy.

RAISING
THE BAR

THE STORY OF CLIF BAR, INC.

White-road journeys are quiet rides. Companies on the red road listen to a lot of noise: the market, shareholders, the board, economic consultants, advisers, and conventional wisdom—all telling them what to do. On our white road, we go about our business with less outside noise. We listen to what our consumers want.

My worst business decisions came when I listened to the noise rather than the quiet of the road.

> **YOUR SHOES HAVE TO FIT IN THE PACK:
> TRAVELING LIGHT**

Jay got off the train in Lucerne to begin our epic trip and boasted, "I fit everything in my pack!" "Sure," I replied, "except for the blue jeans and big tennis shoes you're wearing!" Jay strapped the tennis shoes to the side of his pack. Four days later, a mile up the dirt trail leading to Col Ferret I looked at Jay's bike and asked him, "Dude. Where is your shoe?" A shoe had fallen off as his bike bounced up our rocky gravel road. We descended and found two Swiss German hikers (who earlier said we were crazy to try the pass) holding Jay's shoe. We learned that traveling light means your shoes have to fit in your pack!

JAY (FINDING HIS SHOE)

" I remember how much fun it was leaving to go meet Gary on that first trip.
Before we were refined I just brought over my jeans for my nightly clothes,
which weighed a ton, and tennis shoes that I couldn't fit in the pack. It was
just a blast—laughing hysterically before we left. So I had these shoes that
wouldn't fit inside my pack and these heavy jeans. One day we had prosciutto, melon, and wine in a super-nice, three-star restaurant before riding
over a pass. We head up this road and our tires are bouncing all over the
place on the rocks. We passed hikers. As I caught up to Gary I discovered
that one of my shoes was missing since my bike had been bouncing all over
the place going up this rocky gravel road. We had to ride back down the
road laughing our heads off to find the shoe. We were laughing, the hikers
were laughing. It was so fun. But I never brought tennis shoes again.

We were going over dirt roads before mountain bikes. Our old skinny
wheels just bouncing along these rocky roads. On a trip just a few years
ago we showed a guy a map at a rest stop. We asked him how the road
ahead was. He said, 'You can't do it on those bikes. Mountain bikes
maybe, but not those.' We said, 'Thanks. See you later,' and took off. "

—JAY THOMAS

Traveling Light on the
White-Road Journey

Bike: Ritchey Road Logic
(nineteen pounds)

Pack (eight pounds):
Maps
Bike tools
Capezio dance shoes
Extra socks
Lightweight slacks and shirt (for night)
Boxers
Passport
Credit card and cash
Small notebook and pen
Sunscreen
Toothpaste and brush
Film
Extra cycling clothes (long-sleeved jersey,
    rain jacket and pants, wool cap, tights)

Body: Helmet, Jersey, Cycling shorts, Cycling shoes, Socks,
Energy bars, Camera, Map for the day, Sunglasses

How do you travel light on a bike? Our eight-pound mini-packs held extra cycling clothes for cold and rainy weather, light-weight slacks, shirt, Capezio dance shoes for evening wear, a tool kit, some cash, and a credit card. Every day our joke was, "what are you going to wear for dinner tonight?" Our literal lightness meant that we could explore back roads, mountain passes, and roadless areas that were completely inaccessible to those with heavy panniers. It was easy to load our bikes with wine, baguettes, and cheese when we arrived in a village and made our way to small, one-star hotels.

It's possible to travel more self-sufficiently than we did by carrying everything on your bike—food, a tent, sleeping bag, more clothes, extra bike parts. There are obvious advantages to this option: You won't be caught without warm clothes, food, or a place to sleep. I've taken trips with loaded panniers and support anyone who does. The problem with a weighted-down trip, though, is that you can't travel on the white roads. It's literally impossible to climb a high mountain pass on a single track while loaded down with eighty-pound panniers— and, if you could, descending would be difficult and dangerous. I love road cycling and the beauty of going over a mountain pass on a light bike. For me, "loaded" travel means I am not experiencing the bike and the ride itself.

TOURING HEAVY—1982   TOURING LIGHT—1986

How does a business travel light? First of all it means not overextending. Companies who overextend may have to go to the red road. At Clif Bar we believe that a company (like an individual) lives best when living within its means. One way we keep living within our means is to follow natural consumer demand. By doing this we avoid excessive advertising and marketing budgets. We grow at a rate that we can sustain; we don't overinvest, and we hire at a rate that preserves our corporate culture. Traveling heavy might mean taking on more partners; the more partners the heavier the load. Or it could mean carrying debt. Or people who invest and own a stake and then want to oversee your ride.

Traveling light means we can move fast in any direction and go over any pass we choose.

➤ THE GUIDED TRIP

An alternative to riding with heavy panniers is the guided trip. A guided trip can be a wonderful way to experience the joy of riding in a place you've always dreamed of visiting. Guides carry your belongings in a "sag wagon" that follows behind the cyclists. Guides plan the route and decide where you will eat and sleep, and how far you will travel each day. Someone trails you to fix your flat tire. Even though the cycling is adventurous and fun on a guided tour, you can't explore. If all your needs are met, fewer surprises await you; outcomes are more predictable. Since you travel with your own group, you meet fewer locals. Jay and I didn't have a guide; it made the trip more exhilarating and adventurous for us. We liked finding our own way, hotel, food. We liked having to figure it out. We liked not knowing what would happen next.

TRAVELING WITHOUT A GUIDE IS RISKIER. When we had hypothermia, crawling inside a sag wagon would have been really nice. We didn't have that option. No sag wagon follows behind Clif Bar, either. We don't have the luxury of a "sugar daddy" to bail us out. Many energy bar companies now ride with sag wagons: PowerBar has Nestlé, Odwalla has Coca-Cola, and Balance Bar has Kraft. If they have an unprofitable year their sag wagon can provide a cash infusion.

I think of a venture capital–controlled business as a guided trip. The higher-ups announce, "This is what we are doing,"

RAISING THE BAR

THE STORY OF CLIF BAR, INC.

often without soliciting management or employee opinions. In a company like ours, leaders must make tough business decisions on their own, but they also must listen to their people, including their people's angst. I continually look for ways for people to express their opinions at Clif Bar (like the homework assignments). At Clif I hope to give people room to create their own journeys on our company ride.

> CHANGING COURSE

On our various cycling adventures, Jay and I frequently changed course, rarely sticking to our original plan. On my favorite trip, for example, we planned to ride sixteen hundred miles from Pamplona in Spain to Bassano del Grappa in northern Italy. The first three days out of Pamplona we suffered from the hottest weather I've ever experienced cycling. I became dehydrated and had severe leg cramps (my unfortunate physical trademark!). We rode incredible passes in the Pyrenees, including the Col du Tourmalet and the Col d'Aubisque made famous by the Tour de France. After the third day we realized that the weather was just too hot for northern California guys; we needed to change course. We altered our route, headed north, and had a fantastic trip. We could change course at any moment because we were in full control.

The red-road journey offers few options. The white-road journey creates hundreds of choices. As a private company we can turn right, left, take that route or this pass. We have a freedom not allowed a company that is driven by return on investment and the bottom line. And white-road routes are more interesting! We started out focusing on Luna as a product and then turned a new corner to sponsor LunaFest, an inspiring festival of films by, for, and about women. Proceeds from LunaFest benefit The Breast Cancer Fund, a group that promotes research into the environmental causes of breast cancer. Luna came to represent more than a nutrition bar. Luna also symbolizes women's wellness, power, and a place for women to feel comfortable. Each bar features a personal dedication to women who have touched and inspired us. In like manner, what began as an initiative to use organic ingredients in Clif Bar evolved into promoting wind energy, using recycled boxes, and our company-wide sustainability initiative. Our white-road journey gives us the freedom to change and leads us to hundreds of small and beautiful roads.

For a business, changing course means the flexibility to make unusual business choices; many of which have little to do with the bottom line.

➤ WHITE-ROAD SURPRISES

On the second night of that first adventure with Jay our goal was the village of Gstaad, home to a famous tennis tournament. But when we rode in, Gstaad seemed too touristy for our tastes. We continued riding until we reached a gorgeous high alpine village dotted with small chalets. We decided that we wanted to stay in this delightful village, but we quickly discovered that the town had no hotels. We asked a man if he knew of anyone with rooms to rent. He checked for us and returned with bad news—no rooms in town. As the day darkened, we sat on a bench and consumed a makeshift picnic dinner, figuring we would return to Gstaad. A few minutes later the man returned and said, "You are welcome to stay in my home as guests. I am sorry that the room is in the basement. You won't have to pay." The room turned out to be nicer than that of any three-star hotel, with a television, hot shower, and lots of space. To us it was luxurious indeed. We watched the Tour de France as Greg Lemond took the yellow jersey and later became the first American to win the Tour. Our host then treated us to a four-course meal including raclette (a traditional Swiss cheese dish), wine, vegetables, various meats, dessert, and kirsch. We couldn't believe our good fortune. The following morning our new friend served us breakfast and hugged us good-bye.

I believe this kind of generosity happens when you place yourself in vulnerable positions. We were vulnerable on this trip. We weren't on a planned tour. We weren't in a car. Large panniers didn't carry all the gear that would have allowed us to camp anywhere. Clif Bar Inc. made itself vulnerable by staying private. I think people appreciate Clif's vulnerability and that's why they help us on our journey. People find the best flavors and finest ingredients for us. Others go out of their way to secure the best packaging deals possible. Consumers send us information on sustainability. They know we are not a large entity just trying to make money. Numerous outsiders, similar

to our friend in the Swiss village, have helped Clif during vulnerable periods.

OTHER SURPRISES HAPPEN ON THE WHITE ROAD, surprises that make life special. On our 1989 trip through the Pyrenees, Jay and I rode past castle ruins and through villages that appeared to come from medieval times. One day we stopped for lunch in a tiny village. There were no restaurants or stores, just a small town center and a few homes scattered around the mountainside. As we looked for food a truck pulled up, and the driver started selling cheese and meat to the townspeople from the side of his truck. We stood in line with the locals and bought our cheese and meat. When we asked the man for a baguette, he told us he didn't carry bread and the bread truck had already come and gone. We were content to have any food at all and sat by the fountain in the village center to eat. Across the center we noticed a cute little house with beads covering the door. A woman drew back the beads, stepped outside, and motioned for her son to come out. He held a large half loaf of bread. The young boy walked over to us, handed us the bread and returned to his mother. The woman looked at us and smiled. It felt like a moment out of a beautiful dream. It was a small thing, yet it was one of the most special moments we have ever had on a trip.

On our business journey, many have graced us with loaves of
French bread. I mentioned in Chapter Three how we entertained all our brokers at the privately owned Bloomfield Bakery. Actually, Harold and Bill, who own the bakery, threw
the party for us, charging us a dime on the dollar. They fully
catered the event, using the entire staff from a restaurant that
Harold owned. They erected a large circus tent in the parking
lot, served a wide variety of foods at various stations, and
allowed us to entertain our brokers and employees with music
and marketing and sales presentations. They didn't have to do
this. They knew our struggles, and they supported our values.
They offered the party as a gift to us.

Countless examples like that exist. At a recent bike trade
show, a master swimmer sponsored by the company handed
out Clif Bars to everyone who walked through the door. No one
asked him to, and he wasn't getting paid for it.

Companies on the white road create and attract generosity.

➤ **SPEED**

I have traveled through Europe using most forms of transporta-
tion—bus, train, car, motorcycle, and my own two feet. What I

RAISING THE BAR

THE STORY OF CLIF BAR, INC.

COL DE LA CROIX (SWITZERLAND)

love about being on my bike is the speed—you can ride a hundred miles in a day while moving at a pace that allows you to soak in your surroundings. When you climb you move as slowly as five to ten miles an hour, a great speed for noticing spectacular mountains and valleys. Your body works intensely, but you can still look around. You can talk to your traveling partner, but you are still moving. On the other hand, as you descend, gravity pulls you and you reach exhilarating but natural speeds. Once I sped down a spectacular mountain pass at more than 100 kilometers per hour. (Never again!)

In business if you move too slowly your competition may hit you. But moving at the speed of a French rapid train holds danger as well. If you move too fast you can make decisions that hurt long-term sustainability. To move at the speed of the red road you need money and people to grow quickly. If our company wanted to grow rapidly, we would need to hire a lot of people, which would affect our corporate culture. Hiring at that speed also makes it difficult to hire the right people. If I hired fifty new people at Clif Bar this year it is unlikely that all of them would work out. Moving too fast also might mean bringing on additional funding, which could leverage the company again. Most important, moving too fast means you can't enjoy the ride. Train rides are nice, but on the French fast train you see a village for a split second as you fly by at two hundred

RAISING THE BAR

miles per hour. On our bike rides we enjoyed the scenery and the delights of the culture. I want the same to be true for our business.

➤ HYPOTHERMIA AND KNOWING EXACTLY WHAT TO DO

Jay and I woke to pouring rain on the second morning of our first bike adventure. People had warned us that it might rain a lot, so we figured—when it rains in the Alps you ride. We donned our raingear (which we soon discovered was less than waterproof) and rode up the Grosse Scheidegg, a nine-thou-sand-foot mountain pass in the Swiss Alps. By the time we reached the top of the pass we were soaked to the bones and

shivering with cold. Our speech was slurred and minds slowed down. Given our years of outdoor experience we recognized the signs of hypothermia. Now we faced a four-thousand-foot descent. We could hardly ride during the steep descent and stopped frequently to gain control of our bicycles. I could barely brake or hold on to my handlebars. I could tell my core temperature was dropping to stage one of hypothermia. If your core temperature drops too low you can die. I could tell that Jay was also hypothermic. We were in trouble. We finally made it to the valley town of Grindelwald, Switzerland, and stopped at the first *zimmer* (bed and breakfast) and pounded on the door. A middle-aged Swiss woman opened the door. Jay and I don't speak German and the woman didn't speak English. She looked at us and then, without a word, she yanked us into her home, brought us to the boiler room, told us to remove our clothes, and put each of us into a hot shower. It took us over two hours to get our core temperature back to normal. She fed us hot soup, salami, cheese, and bread. When the weather cleared later that afternoon she hugged us and sent us on our way.

I LEARNED TWO LESSONS FROM OUR EXPERIENCE: Be prepared and act decisively. We didn't have the right gear and we didn't know how far it was from the mountain pass to our first shelter. If we had been on a guided trip we would have had access to extra gear from the sag wagon; on a red road we would have found shelter more quickly. Since we were on the white road we needed to be better prepared. The woman who took us in taught me the second lesson. She asked no questions. She took one look at us, knew exactly what was needed, and acted. Most likely she had seen mountain climbers come off the Eiger or the Jungfrau in various stages of hypothermia. A business on

RAISING THE BAR

THE STORY OF CLIF BAR, INC.

the white road doesn't have backup and needs to be well prepared for whatever might come. All businesses, white or red, can create strategic plans forever, but sometimes executive decisions need to be made and action taken without any hesitation. For a company that is not heavily funded like ours, decisive execution must be nearly flawless.

➤ KEEPING YOUR TOOLS IN SHAPE

Heading over the St. Gotthard pass out of Switzerland into Italy, I was hot, dehydrated, and irritable. It didn't help my mood that I was hearing a clicking sound with each stroke of the pedal. I knew something was wrong with my bike but couldn't figure it out. Finally, halfway up the pass I discovered the culprit: a broken link in my chain. Fortunately I had the right bike tool to repair it. But I realized I hadn't made sure that my major "tool"—the bicycle—was in perfect condition *before* we set out. I started the trip with a chain that had ten thousand miles of wear on it. Of course it would break. A trip like ours requires that all equipment be in perfect condition. Both bikes and bodies need to be in top shape. I repaired my bike on the road that day but from then on we made sure that our bikes were finely tuned. There are bike shops in Europe, but that won't help when you are thirty miles from town or need repairs on a Sunday.

IN BUSINESS ALL YOUR TOOLS MUST BE IN TOP FORM. All legal contracts, employment policies, employee handbooks, Web sites, written materials, need to be in perfect shape. Computer systems must be right. Clif learned by making many mistakes, like having the wrong software for a job. Fixing that cost us needless stress and money. We should have moved into a better building two years before we did. A white-road business can't afford broken links!

> SEND THAT TELEGRAM

As Jay and I left the Lucerne train station on the first day, I asked him, "So, how much money did you bring?" I figured that we needed money for a twelve- to fourteen-day trip. At the time I was living hand-to-mouth; I brought $400 and a credit card. I was hoping that Jay could supplement my stash significantly. Jay answered, "Eighty dollars." I panicked. "Jay, $80 divided by fourteen days is $6 a day. This is not going to work." There we were in Europe with a serious money problem. We decided to telegraph Joe Hazelby, a pilot flying out of Berlin and the father of Jay's best friend in high school. We hadn't talked to Joe in four years. The first draft of our telegram (this was 1986, before e-mail) was friendly. "Hi Joe. Haven't seen you in a long time. How are you doing?" We quickly realized that every word costs money. The friendly version would set us back $20, a quarter of Jay's money. We finally sent a $5 telegram: **"Joe. Need money. Send to Chamonix Post. On bike trip. Jay and Gary."**

We took off from Lucerne with $475 and a credit card that maxed out at $450. We arrived in Chamonix three days later, the same day I hit my record for number of espressos consumed in one day—eleven—a record I never want to break. The caffeine level added to my anxiety over the money. I had given up. Even if Joe weren't insulted, the chances of getting the money seemed slim to me. I guarded our bicycles while Jay went to check the Post. A few minutes later I watched Jay cross the

RAISING THE BAR

THE STORY OF CLIF BAR, INC.

square looking like a football player who had just scored a touchdown. Joe sent us $250!

Yes, we were irresponsible youths, but I learned a lesson from this experience. On the white road you may have to find creative ways to fund your business. No one thought we could find the money to buy out my business partner. We explored countless alternatives and got creative. The process was something like sending telegrams out to people you hadn't seen in four years. Anyone who wants to stay on the white road needs to figure out how many telegrams they can send. I talk to many small business owners who struggle to find funding to grow their businesses. Typically they only explore conventional means of funding, such as venture capital, other investors, or bank loans. They also need the creativity to find their own Joe Hazelby!

➤ PUSHING HARD AND LOVING IT

This ain't no weenie roast.

—JAY THOMAS

On our trip through the Pyrenees from Spain to France Jay and I rode two 120-mile days, this after riding 800 miles in eight days. We could have stopped at the seventy- or eighty-mile mark each

**NICK, RESTING
BEFORE DINNER**
(VAL GARDENA, 1992)

THE STORY OF CLIF BAR, INC.

RAISING THE BAR

day, but we wanted to return to villages that we knew were especially beautiful. Aesthetic goals motivated us—good food, incredible beauty, and famous passes like Col du Galibier, Col du Madeleine, and Col du Izord. We rode in the rain and cold. We pushed hard, facing fourteen thousand feet of climbing each day. On our own with no sag wagon to offer us a ride, we pushed hard to make it. Each morning we woke up wondering if we could even walk to breakfast, much less get on our bikes and ride again. After three or four espressos, juice, fifteen hundred calories of bread, jam, and cheese, we would say to each other, "Let's go." Those 120-mile days remain some of my most memorable rides.

Our decision to "go organic" pushed us at Clif Bar. I wanted Clif to be officially organic by January 2003. We accomplished our goal by Fall 2002. Analyzing every ingredient in Clif Bars was tough going. We assessed hundreds of ingredients. In spite of the difficult process, people were inspired and worked extraordinarily hard. Just as Jay and I knew the village we wanted to reach, even if it meant pedaling fifty extra miles, people were willing to work harder to get to the place where they wanted Clif Bar to be—a company that used organic ingredients.

The cycling trips I describe in this chapter are difficult. They are fun and adventurous but demand careful preparation and a willingness to take risks. What gets you through them is the sheer love and passion for the journey. You have to love every part of the trip—the hard work, the preparation, the adventure. Since you might pedal eight to twelve hours a day for twenty-one days you have to love being on your bike.

I couldn't continue on the Clif Bar journey just because I felt it was the right thing to do (although I do). I do it because I love it. If you are going to be self-funded, take huge risks, and work really hard, it must be out of desire. I couldn't survive a white-road bike trip or white-road business journey without that underlying passion.

The white road is the entrepreneur's path, full of passion and adventure.

› FACTS NOT FICTION, OR, I NEVER GOLFED WITH ARNOLD PALMER

The kind of adventure travel I'm describing places extreme stress on the body. If you bonk on a red road or on a guided trip you can get a ride to your destination. On the white-road journey what gets you from Point A to Point B is you. Honesty is critical. If you need to recover, that is what you have to do. You can't fake it. At times Jay or I would say, "I have to take a day off. I have to rest. If I go another day I'm going to go crazy." We couldn't make excuses to protect our egos. We had to be honest with each other. Companies on the red road, the Enrons of the world, struggle with honesty. Why does this occur more on the red than the white road? Maybe those of us on the white road feel the effects of dishonesty more immediately and directly.

Maybe it's easier to see when people are not truthful in an intimate group. I would rather hear an employee say, "This is too hard," than see someone try to fake it.

I think you can be dishonest in a larger corporation and get away with it for a long time, possibly for an entire career. But even small companies like Clif deal with dishonesty. My brother and our director of operations called me into the office of one of our employees. They were super excited. "Tell him, tell him," they said. The employee said, "I got you into the Pro Am of the Fred Meyer Challenge (a senior tournament with big names like Tom Watson and Jack Nicklaus). Your foursome is our broker, the CEO of Fred Meyer, and Arnold Palmer." Everyone knows I love golf. I couldn't believe it and we all danced around the office high-fiving each other. Think about it. Twenty-five million golfers in the country and only a few have played with Arnold Palmer. Later, I ran into our broker at a trade show in Chicago. He asked, "Hey, are you coming to the Fred Meyer Challenge?" I answered, "Of course. I'm golfing in the Pro Am with you, the CEO of Fred Meyer, and Arnold Palmer. I can't wait!" He looked at me like I had lost my mind. When he heard of the promise, the broker asked, "So, how is the guy going to get out of that one?" It turned out that he'd built a house of cards using the most common form of business dishonesty: exaggeration. Exaggeration seems endemic to business. In

RAISING THE BAR

THE STORY OF CLIF BAR, INC.

WHITE ROAD VERSUS RED ROAD

" The red road is predictable, a known entity, safe, and conservative. It gets the traveler to the destination in what might be referred to as the most efficient manner. We know how far it is, and how long it will take. The map is marked with mileage and approximate travel time. There is generally little in the way of risk, and consequently, a parallel lack of reward.

The white road is just the opposite. It is the road less traveled. It is an unknown entity, unpredictable, and there may be danger and hardship along the way. We don't know how long the road is, and even when we do, we can't predict time because of the difficulty of travel over the unknown route. Most important, there is likely to be adventure. Adventure, by definition, implies some level of hardship or danger. But along with this hardship or danger, there is often reward. The reward is a sense of accomplishment—the joy and beauty of the journey along the road less traveled.

The dictionary defines adventure in the following way: *1—the encountering of danger. 2—a daring, hazardous undertaking. 3—an unusual, stirring experience, often of a romantic nature. 4—a venture or speculation in business or finance.*

Of particular interest and relevance here are 3 and 4. An adventure (the white road) is often a 'stirring' experience, and romantic, not necessarily as the word

Col du Galibier

pertains to human relationships, but to how the traveler relates to the beauty and peril of the surrounding world.

Additionally, the definition has relevance in the business sense. Clif Bar's vision, and our business plan, is an adventure, definitely the white road. As such, it is sometimes more difficult, and the risks are present, though in this case it is not bodily harm that we are concerned with. Rather it is our success in the business world, our ability to compete and succeed using our unorthodox mode of travel (business plan), that is, the white road. When we succeed, the rewards make the effort worthwhile and we continue on, further impassioned by our accomplishments.

There are those who prefer the easy road, and there are those who prefer a more interesting, albeit much harder, journey. The white-road traveler enjoys and thrives on the adventure, the peril, the beauty, and the reward. Without these things to feed the soul, the white-road traveler feels empty and unfulfilled.

The red-road traveler prefers the easier and more predictable way to reach the destination. The journey, and the adventure associated with this journey, is not important. The red-road traveler desires to reach the destination with the least amount of effort and peril. „

–PAUL MCKENZIE, DIRECTOR OF LUNA CHIX

photo by Graham Watson

addition to promising a golf foursome with Arnold Palmer, this employee habitually rounded numbers up and overprojected sales. He also rounded up expense reports. Exaggerating, overprojecting, making promises that can't be fulfilled, may seem like strategies to protect the business, the job, yourself. Yet in the end, like a house of cards, it fails. It always costs. It cost this employee his job as soon as the pattern became clear.

A white-road bicycle trip cannot be built on a facade. Neither can a business. Honesty and clarity work best.

➤ FINDING A ROUTE WHERE THERE ISN'T ONE

The year following my first ride with Jay we brought two friends on a similar trip. We knew what to do. We had the right maps. We didn't have a guidebook. On the fourth day of our trip we needed to get to the base of the Stelvio in northern Italy. According to the map, the only way was by red road, which meant lots of cars, trucks, exhaust, and objective danger. We hated red roads, yet we conceded there didn't seem to be an alternative. As Jay sipped his beer and studied the map, he found a white road that dead-ended on the Austrian border, then a roadless three-thousand-foot pass and a white road on the other side dropping into Italy. Jay and I knew from our Col Ferret experience the previous year that this route might go, although it certainly wasn't the fastest way to the base of the Stelvio. We could take the red road and make it to the top of the pass in one day. Jay's proposed route would take us an extra day, and we didn't even know if it was possible. We discussed our options that night. Jay and I wanted to attempt the combined white-road/roadless route. Clem, an experienced rock climber, questioned us closely, and then decided to go with us. Our friend Michael, although an adventurous person, had never rock or mountain climbed. He opted for the red road and planned to meet his misguided companions the following evening in a small village at the base of the Stelvio.

Early the next morning the three of us headed up an incredible valley, enjoying classic Austrian countryside and villages along the way. Even though it was possible that late afternoon would find us backtracking around the entire mountain, we rode enjoying the moment, not thinking about the outcome. During our stop for lunch at a high mountain chalet and restaurant, we met an enthusiastic seventy-two-year-old Irishwoman leading a group of tourists. Since she had led numerous tours in the area, we pulled out a map, laid it on a table, pointed to where we wanted to go, and asked, "Do you think this will go?" Without hesitation she said, "Oh yes, that will go. This is such a good adventure you are doing. I wish I could go with you." Buoyed by her positive attitude, we decided to go for it.

RAISING THE BAR

THE STORY OF CLIF BAR, INC.

"Oh yes, this will go . . .
I wish I could go with you."

We met an enthusiastic 72-year-old Irish woman leading a tour group

We took a *leap of faith*. Even though our new friend was confident and we were experienced mountain climbers, we didn't really know if the path would go. We had no climbing gear. We didn't have ropes. We might reach the top and find a thousand-foot drop.

Off we went, still riding on a paved road. We met other cyclists enjoying a day trip up and back on our road. They asked us where we were going; we answered, "Over the pass." "What pass?" they asked. Cyclists who lived in the area told us, "There is no pass there. That route doesn't go. You will find glaciers, crevasses." They thought we were crazy.

RAISING THE BAR

THE STORY OF CLIF BAR, INC.

Finally we left the road. We would have to ascend our pass on foot, carrying our bicycles over snowfields. We couldn't walk that kind of terrain in our cycling shoes and the only other shoes we had with us were Capezio dance shoes. We carried dance shoes because they were flat, light, and easy to pack. But they don't make for good hiking or climbing in the snow. How to turn lightweight dance shoes into waterproof mountain boots? We put plastic bags over our feet and—voilà!—lightweight, waterproof climbing shoes. I'd done this often, climbing mountain passes in the Alps, the Sierra, in Nepal, but never carrying a bike and walking in Capezio dance shoes! We put our bikes over our backs and hiked up at least two thousand feet (the

pass was at about eleven thousand feet). We encountered
crevasses, but fortunately they were minor. We continued
ascending. A pass is *never* where you think it is, and several
false passes fooled us on our long trek up the mountain. We
reached the top of the more obvious of two passes, peered over
into thin air and a thousand-foot drop. No go. We descended
and tried another pass that proved to be the official pass,
marked by a wooden crucifix.

"A pass is **never** where you think it is."

We celebrated, relieved that we had discovered the pass. Yet it was late in the day and we had to get down the other side and then ride twenty miles on the main road to meet Michael. We had a huge descent of nearly four thousand feet facing us, and the path down held snow for at least fifteen hundred feet. We were getting cold, had little food, no stove to melt snow for water, and we were in danger of slipping down the mountain in our dance shoes. I thought about glissading, the technique where you essentially ski down a snow slope on climbing boots. There were two problems: We needed ice axes and how were we going to get our bikes to glissade with us? If Capezio dance shoes could serve as climbing shoes, why couldn't a bicycle double as an ice axe? I ended up sticking my right armpit on top of the bike seat and holding the handlebars with both hands. I stuck out my feet like a water skier and started down the hill. We glissaded down 1,500 vertical feet on a twenty- to thirty-degree slope using our bicycles for balance and as makeshift ice axes. We flew at a rate of about fifteen to twenty kilometers per hour on the snow (according to my bike computer). Glissading felt like pure joy after all our hard work.

After the snow ended, we found ourselves on a single-track trail. Riding on the trail we helped each other cross raging streams, jumping from rock to rock while passing our bikes. At one point we rode across a field of wildflowers; the blooms

RAISING THE BAR

THE STORY OF CLIF BAR, INC.

came up to our knees. It felt like we were floating on flowers. We emerged onto a desolate road and waved at a lone farmer. He looked at us as if we had just landed from Mars. We were now on paved road and in Italy, thoroughly exhausted. By 7 P.M. we found a store, ate voraciously, rode fifteen more miles and found a place to sleep. We didn't meet up with Michael that night. We found him the following morning eight kilometers up the road. From that point on he joined us on the white roads.

No apparent alternative existed to the red road. Yet we found a pass and one of the greatest adventures of our lives. Often companies on the red road can't see any alternatives to conven-

tional ways of formulating products, structuring organizations, funding, advertising, sales, or marketing. In 2000 I couldn't see any alternative to selling Clif Bar Inc. Obviously, there were alternatives.

Another example with "no apparent alternative" led us to one of the initiatives I am most proud of—the Beyond the Podium campaign and award. Clif Bar sponsors the United States Postal Service (USPS) Pro Cycling Team, which participates in all the big tours like the Tour de France. A few years ago I received a call from Lance Armstrong's agent. PowerBar had just offered Lance $400,000 a year for three years. Even though we were the exclusive energy bar sponsors of the USPS Pro Cycling Team, Lance planned to take the PowerBar deal unless we matched it. This shocked people at Clif Bar, but they were emphatic, "Just pay him. We don't have an alternative." Even though it was over ten times our current contract, I almost did pay him. I returned to the office after reflecting for five days and told everyone, "I'm not going to do it. I don't know what we are going to do but there has to be a way to make this work." In the end we remained the sponsor of the USPS Pro Cycling Team (a little awkward since PowerBar sponsors Lance). We created an alternative campaign, Beyond the Podium, which became the talk of the bicycle industry. Beyond the Podium honors the teammates, the *domestiques* as they are called—the guys who ride for Lance, who get him to the finish line, and help him win the race. The *domestiques* are unsung heroes. Clif is the first sponsor in the history of cycling to honor the *domestiques* with an award like Beyond the Podium. People vote for the most valuable *domestique,* who receives a cash prize from Clif Bar

"Every day at Clif Bar,
as we head up the next pass
wondering if it will go,
we make a leap of faith."

and is honored at an award ceremony at the annual InterBike Show. As we say in our campaign, without the *domestiques* there would be no glory.

➤ LEAP OF FAITH

I enjoyed more than twenty tours and twenty thousand cycling miles over the next fifteen years. They brought together my varied passions—cycling, climbing, aesthetics, food, good people, travel. More important, they were adventures—they were leaps of faith like our ride over a snowy pass. Those journeys also shaped my philosophy of life, the philosophy underlying how I want to own and run a business. Since that first trip the white road/red road metaphor has helped me keep Clif on the white road. Every day we face forks in the road. Every day we have to take leaps of faith. Defaulting on any of the elements listed in this chapter could lead the company off the white road. When I first told the white road/red road story at a Thursday Morning Meeting, someone said, "We face those kinds of decisions daily, whether it is about marketing, product, advertising, or finance." If we consistently make wrong decisions we will move to the red road and become a different company.

I believe we have kept Clif Bar on the white road. The defining moment for me was whether or not I would hop off the road altogether and sell the company. All paths seemed to lead to that red road. I decided to keep the company private. Choosing the white-road/roadless pass was a leap of faith. We didn't know if it would work. Choosing to walk away from the money and go into debt was a leap of faith. Companies that remain self-funded, that stay private, that compete against the "big guys," and that need people to believe in them—those companies need huge leaps of faith.

EVERY DAY AT CLIF BAR, AS WE HEAD UP THE NEXT PASS WONDERING IF IT WILL GO, WE MAKE A LEAP OF FAITH.

CHAPTER 5

TALES FROM THE ROAD

(NINE LESSONS AND A LOVE STORY)

I believe that life experiences teach you philosophies and values, and your philosophies and values shape how you deal with risk, how you treat people, and how you feel about money. In other words, I believe entrepreneurs bring their life stories into business. Right now my life stories center around Clif Bar. In this chapter I tell tales from other defining moments in my life—stories from my youth and more recent adventures that have influenced my business (and life) values.

➤ LESSON ONE: TEAMWORK—MY CINDERELLA STORY

Team sports were common in the suburbs of northern California where I grew up. I loved sports and gained a lot from playing them. Today I firmly believe that playing sports benefits all kids, especially young girls, and regret that it has taken us so long to embrace sports for girls. Up through high school I played soccer, baseball, football; I ran cross-country and played tennis. When I entered Ohlone Junior College I decided to play

OHLONE COLLEGE SOCCER TEAM: PREGAME WARMUP. —MARK CANTLEY

soccer. Although I wasn't a super-skilled player, I worked hard, moved quickly, and provided solid defense. Our team claimed no star players, but we enjoyed being together and benefited from an amazing coach, Frank Mangiola. Frank emphasized teamwork in a way I had never experienced, and he made me view soccer in a new light. Our games didn't attract hundreds of people: We knew this wasn't the World Cup! But that didn't stop us from loving the game with a passion and working together as a team.

Our team sneaked into the playoffs through a freak three-way tie in our division. Surprisingly we beat both of the other teams and won the division. We moved up to the Northern California State Cup finals and faced De Anza College, the team ranked fourth in the national junior college division. Our team wasn't even ranked during the season! To say we were underdogs gives us too much credit.

Before a game starts, teams warm up. The warm-up area becomes a kind of sacred ground, the half of the field that the other team won't enter out of respect. As we warmed up before the big game, the other team started running in a circle around us, taunting us, and trying to intimidate us by consciously invading our warm-up space. Our coach never acknowledged them. He calmly told us, "Don't respond." It was a powerful moment: We didn't give in to our anger; we stayed calm and focused. We played our hearts out, better than we had ever played. We played as one person. We could pass with our eyes closed and connect with a teammate. We beat them two to one. I was shocked that we won. How could we have beaten that team? It was our Cinderella story.

At Clif Bar, we faced our own De Anza/Ohlone College match-up in 1997. Our all-natural energy bar had taken market share from PowerBar for several years. PowerBar eventually responded by introducing Harvest Bar, a product made of whole grains with a texture similar to Clif Bar. It also planned on spending millions of dollars introducing the product. Rumor had it that the product boasted the code name "Clif Killer." People at Clif were nervous and anxious; we felt as if we were in the warm-up zone being circled by the big guys! I told the company my Cinderella Story and what coach Mangiola told us: "Keep playing our own game." And we did. PowerBar's Harvest Bar didn't kill Clif. Years later Clif's strong teamwork helps the Clif brand remain strong and grow.

What I've learned is that when we don't work as a team it shows up in bad results and low morale. In the business world, work too often becomes compartmentalized, leading to a distorted concept of teamwork: You do your job, I do my job, and somehow that equals performance and teamwork. At Clif, our organizational structure backs our belief in teamwork. I also learned that no matter what the challenge, "keep playing your own game": stick to your core competencies.

Clif Bar holds the twin advantages of great people and great team playing—we can move together quickly to create our own Cinderella stories.

> LESSON TWO: HAVE THE TIME OF YOUR LIFE

After I finished college I worked several years for Sierra Treks, a wilderness program modeled after Outward Bound. It was my favorite job prior to Clif Bar. We brought people of all ages to the mountains for intense trips ranging from ten to eighteen days. We taught wilderness and climbing skills and minimum-impact camping, and we tried to instill a love for the environment in others. We guided trips through the Sierra Nevada, the Trinity Alps, the Oregon and Washington Cascades, Joshua Tree National Monument, and other mountain ranges. The job had me doing everything that I loved to do. I hiked, climbed, roamed the mountains, and got to sleep outside for 130 days a year!

The best part of the job was the people. My coworkers and I happily wandered the mountains for $100 a month. Money didn't matter. We loved being together and believed passionately in what we were doing. We climbed, laughed, hiked, and learned together. To this day my fellow mountain guides are some of my closest friends, and although I started with Sierra Treks more than twenty-five years ago, when we get together, it feels like yesterday. We didn't just work together; we shared life adventures. I traveled in Nepal and India with Sheila. I climbed and hiked in Europe with Julie. I climbed Half Dome with Bruce. I backcountry skied and camped with Lois.

Dave Willis, the director of Sierra Treks, possessed an uncanny ability to hire the right people. He selected people for mountain skills, but also for people skills, values, and who they were. As a

SIERRA TREKS
STAFF.
—GARY ERICKSON

consequence, we savored every minute together. We didn't care
what we were doing. We could be packing food for a trip, cleaning out a horse stall, repairing backpacks—you name it—and
have an incredible time. We enjoyed being around each other
and believed in what we were doing. We planned other climbing
trips between our Treks trips, constantly figuring out ways to
be together in the wilderness.

I try to create that atmosphere at Clif Bar. I ask myself, "Why
can't a business be like that? Why can't one reason that you
come to work be that you really like the people—you enjoy working, being together, and learning from each other?" At Sierra
Treks the right mix of people was central; the same is true for
Clif Bar. Skills are important, of course, but just as at Treks,
at Clif Bar, people are hired for their skills and for who they
are. At Sierra Treks, I had climbing skills but I worked alongside academics, yet I never felt intimidated by anyone. We
shared each other's strengths and learned from each other.
The same is true at Clif; people value their colleagues' many
talents. The diversity of people at Clif Bar has created an eclec-
tic, creative atmosphere.

Clif Bar makes recreating together available, but not forced. Recreating together may include a rock-climbing weekend, working with Habitat for Humanity, or ski trips. People at Clif Bar climb together, sail together, ride bikes together. Sometimes this occurs through a company event, but most of the time it happens informally. People amaze me by volunteering for Clif events. For example, when we cook a dinner in our commercial kitchen for the sales team, ten people may volunteer just so they can hang out and cook together.

Every day I witness Clif people enjoying and learning from each other. They believe in what they are doing and respect each other—a powerful combination.

➤ LESSON THREE: MAINTAIN COMPOSURE, OR, DARTH VADER'S REVENGE

I've climbed in the Alps and all over the United States and trekked in the Himalayas, but to me no climbing spot is as dramatic or as beautiful as Tuolumne Meadows in the high Sierra of California. Tuolumne doesn't boast multi-day climbs, yet any climber in the world will tell you that it's one of the scariest places to climb, especially to lead. In Chapter One I described the type of belaying that protects climbers who follow the lead. Protecting, for the lead climber, carries more risk. The lead

TUOLOMNE ROCK CLIMBING.
—JAY THOMAS

climber ascends, placing pieces of protection in the rock or using preexisting protection, such as pitons driven into cracks or bolts drilled into rock faces. The climber clips the rope into the protection with a carabiner and continues climbing. In a sense, as lead you create your protection as you go. If you fall while leading, you plummet at least twice the distance from your last piece of protection. If you are ten feet above your protection, you may fall twenty-five feet. Tuolumne is famous for long stretches of rock where protecting is difficult.

My buddies and I loved Tuolumne, despite the difficulties of protecting our climbs. Every summer weekend would find us climbing Tuolumne walls, and we grew accustomed to the Tuolumne style of climbing, where we would face twenty, thirty, forty, sometimes sixty-foot falls. European friends who came to Tuolumne sometimes refused to climb. They were accustomed to close protection and short falls. Bouncing and scraping down a rock wall didn't strike them as particularly enjoyable!

One gorgeous Tuolumne summer day, Jay and I decided to climb Darth Vader's Revenge, a beautiful multi-pitch climb. (A *pitch* is a section of a climb.) The climb was five pitches long, about 450 feet. The first pitches were difficult, rated up to 5.10a, with long stretches between protection. (Climbs are rated by a number system, with the most difficult climbs in the 5.10a–5.14d range.) Jay led the scary second-to-last pitch, and, as I waited below, I wondered what was taking him so long. When I climbed up to him I thanked God that I hadn't led that pitch. It was difficult and poorly protected. The final pitch, which I would lead, was rated less difficult so I thought I'd gotten off easy. The first moves had me climbing a small overhang. I couldn't see Jay

THE STORY OF CLIF BAR, INC.

RAISING THE BAR

anymore. From the overhang to the top of the climb was 120 feet. Although it was rated lower than the previous pitch, the rock was flat with few features, there were no bolts, and the wind was blowing hard. For 120 feet there was nowhere to place protection. If I fell near the top of the climb, I would fall at least 240 feet, certainly to my death. I yelled at Jay who could barely hear me over the sound of the wind. He laughed and shouted back, "Dude. Please don't pancake on me. I don't want to deal with a pancake." Freaking out was not an option. I needed to remain smooth and focused. I kept climbing, one step at a time. I made it to the top and belayed Jay up the face. Just another day of climbing in Tuolumne Meadows!

I learned from Darth Vader's Revenge, and hundreds of other climbs, to maintain composure. You shouldn't lose your composure in business, either. I think this is especially true for entrepreneurs, but it applies to all leaders. It doesn't work to freak out. It doesn't pay. No matter how tense a situation, you need to stay composed and make one move at a time. On a climb you must not look too far ahead—if you try to map out every move to the top, you'll take your attention away from the move you're making at that moment. And that's a good recipe for a fall. Good climbers only plan a few moves ahead. After all, if you don't know the climb, you can't really plan the whole route. In business, how can you know the whole climb ahead of time? You can't focus on the top, or the red-road goal. You can only focus on the next few moves.

I needed composure during the intense negotiations that ensued after my partner told me that I had to buy her out. Bruce Lymburn, my attorney, wisely advised me to bite my tongue

RAISING THE BAR

THE STORY OF CLIF BAR, INC.

RAISING THE BAR

THE STORY OF CLIF BAR, INC.

" I've always thought of climbing as a way of life. Seeking balance with nature ultimately seemed to be the key for any successful climb. Learning to feel with the senses to become more aware of the real world, the natural world, our life source. These kinds of feelings come from a deep respect for all of life, as it has been shown to me climbing and living in Yosemite.

The people at Clif Bar turn their business into a way of life. All this gives me hope to continue my own journey to discover the potential we all have to wake up our spirit and just do something good for ourselves and the whole wide world. "

—RON KAUK, CLIMBER

RON KAUK CLIMBING.
—MARK CHAPMAN

RAISING THE BAR

THE STORY OF CLIF BAR, INC.

and remain calm no matter what happened. In climbing you need to understand the consequences of your fall but can't focus on falling; you need to know exactly where the top is, but you can't get ahead of yourself. I'd begun the negotiations assuming that there would be logical protection, a way to work through our differences. I never planned on a solo business climb without protection. When it became clear that I had no logical protection, the consequences of this particular business fall zoomed into focus: it might mean that the company would need to be dissolved. I also found that I couldn't think about what it would be like if I owned the company 100 percent. The negotiations demanded literally hundreds of moves. I realized that I could only make one or two moves at a time. I needed to block thinking of a business fall or of getting to the top.

Business is stressful. A good leader remains composed, stays in the moment, focuses on one good move, then the next. No matter how radical the fall you face, keep your cool.

> LESSON FOUR: ON ICE, SHAKEN BUT NOT STIRRED

Another time that I climbed with a friend, things got even dicier. On a beautiful fall morning in 1979, my friend Bruce Hendricks and I left camp to climb North Peak in Yosemite. We approached our route, an eight-hundred-foot snow and ice chute wedged between two rock faces with a fifty-degree pitch, full of confidence. After all, we had climbed and guided in the Sierra Nevada all summer; the climb should be a walk in the park.

We started climbing on hard snow and our ice tools sunk into the snow nicely. Bruce and I traded leads, and the climbing felt

ICE CLIMBING ON NORTH PEAK.
—GARY ERICKSON

ICE CLIMBING ON
NORTH PEAK.
—BRUCE HENDRICKS

easy and secure. Three hundred feet up the chute, the surface changed from snow to ice. The fun was beginning! It was my turn to lead and I climbed out onto solid ice. My tools and the teeth of my crampons (a steel frame with spikes attached to boots for ice climbing) barely penetrated the icy surface. I cruised up ninety feet without placing any protection in the rock face to my left. If I fell, I would plummet 180 feet to a rock wall, injuring both my belayer (Bruce belayed old-style by wrapping the rope around his waist) and myself. I felt confident, however, and moved smoothly toward my belay station.

I noticed one of my crampons was loose, which made it more difficult to kick into the ice to get a solid footing. Not a problem, I thought, I still had two ice axes in the ice and a tightly strapped crampon on my other boot. (Climbers always try to have at least three points of contact on ice or rock at all times.) As I swung my ice axe for another placement, the pick hit the hard surface, jumped back, and flew out of my hand—landing two hundred feet below me. Looking down to where the axe lay, I saw the fate that awaited me if I fell, but hey, I thought, I still had my three points of contact. Then the loose crampon came off and dangled around my ankle. I unhooked it carefully and threw it in a hole between rock and ice to my left. I was now climbing with two points of contact. My hand without the ice axe and foot without the crampon were useless against the hard ice. I had to balance on the icy surface and try to move, while hanging onto one ice axe or one crampon.

ALL MY WEIGHT RESTED ON ONE ARM AND ONE LEG. I realized that soon I would be fatigued and experience sewing machine leg, the twitching that occurs on climbs when isometric pressure mounts. If that happened, my foot would surely come flying out and I couldn't afford that. A fall began to look possible. I had to move.

If I could traverse across ten feet of icy surface I would reach a rock wall where I could put in protection. I needed to quickly develop a new climbing technique, one that enabled me to traverse a fifty-degree ice chute with only one ice axe and one crampon. I placed my axe into the ice, hung on to it with both hands, and carefully removed my foot. I kicked my foot with the crampon into the ice and carefully removed my axe. This was incredibly scary. I had to balance on one foot, and any shift in weight could cause me to fall to my death. I repeated the moves several times and began to believe that I could make it to the safety of the rock wall, if I stayed focused. I finally reached the rock wall, placed protection in a crack and continued to climb using a hybrid rock-ice technique, climbing the ice to my right with axe and crampon, and climbing rock to my left until I reached a ledge fifteen feet above me where I could belay Bruce. Fortunately, the rest of the climb was less eventful, and we returned to camp after retrieving the dropped ice axe.

I use three words to talk about what I learned from that climbing story: *attentive, adaptive,* and *action.* I wasn't *attentive* on the climb. I hadn't properly strapped on my crampon, I didn't have a leash on my ice axe, I didn't adequately protect the climb, and I hadn't anticipated changes in the icy surface. When it all went wrong, I needed to *adapt* quickly. Finally, I needed to take *action* to make it to safety.

Clif Bar faced its own version of the ice chute story in 2003. We missed our sales projections for the first eight months, and our profit dropped by 26 percent. Luna, which experienced 30 percent growth in 2002, saw its sales plummet to 10 percent below the previous year's sales—revenues fell 20 percent below budget. Luna was moving backward! Mojo, projected to reach $9 million in sales, barely made $1.5 million. Accustomed to near-exponential growth year after year, we were shocked to see company revenues flatten and go downhill, especially in such a short span of time. People were still passionate and working hard, but their efforts didn't yield the customary stellar success. Morale suffered and anxiety grew. Clif Bar had dropped an ice axe, lost its crampon, and now faced a big fall.

What had happened? After eleven years of stellar revenue growth and consistently solid profit margins, why were we so off? How could we move Clif back to the rock?

ATTENTIVE: WE ASKED REALLY HARD QUESTIONS AND FACED THE FACTS. We had rested on our laurels and hadn't prepared adequately for 2003 or 2004. We hadn't attended to changes in the market or listened carefully enough to our consumers. Our two largest competitors, Nestlé with PowerBar and Kraft with Balance Bar, spent big money on advertising and promotion, and we felt the effects. Certain diets grew in popularity, including the Atkins and South Beach diets, leading to new eating trends. A new wave of players entered the category. We had our best financial year in 2002, but in 2003 we launched no new products and only a few new flavors for existing brands. We had no protection in place to secure our growth and commitment to innovation.

ADAPTIVE: HOW DO WE MOVE FORWARD? Halfway through 2003, I delivered the "Blessings in Disguise" speech to the company. I said that our downturn was a blessing because it gave us the opportunity to take a judicious look at our company. We analyzed each piece of our business model. We looked at moves that would support our long-term desire to remain independent and self-fund our growth.

ACTION: TAKE THE RISK. We made radical changes in the company. We hired new people, keeping in mind the specific skills needed to make our move to the next level. We reorganized based on supporting our overall vision (the Five Aspirations described in Chapter Seven) rather than individual departments. We initiated a rebirth of product innovation, committing ourselves to an ongoing pipeline of new products. We became more decisive in our execution of plans. Did it all turn around immediately? No. It took months before we saw results.

We continue to climb "hybrid," striving to be attentive, adaptive, and prepared for action. At all times companies need to be ready to face the facts, explore options, and move!

➤ LESSON FIVE: PROSCIUTTO AND VINO

I'd never stepped a foot outside the United States. I longed to trek and climb in the Himalayas and Europe; I wanted to travel to the Middle East. In 1981, I decided to make it happen and held down three jobs to save money for a trip: I parked cars at North Beach Restaurant in San Francisco, mounted and tuned skis, and hammered nails and installed insulation for a building contractor. I worked ten to fourteen hours a day for twelve months and saved close to $20,000. At last I was ready to take off on a year-long, round-the-world trekking, climbing, and biking adventure.

I left the United States just after New Year's Day in 1982 loaded down with skis, backpack, mountain climbing gear, and a bicycle. I flew to Munich, Germany, where my friend Graig Flach was kind enough to provide me (or more accurately, my gear!) with a base. The plan was to return to Germany between trips to pick up gear for the next climbing, cycling, or skiing adventure. The moment I landed in Germany I knew this would be the trip of my life. I entered a smoky coffee shop with Graig and listened to German being spoken all around me. Later that night I savored my first *weiss* beer in a beer hall. I relished every drop.

My cousin John and I grew up skiing and always dreamed of skiing in the Alps. So we'd planned for him to join me for the first adventure of my trip: we skied in the Austrian Alps and in Italy. It was fantastic. On a tram in Austria a group of Italians overheard us speaking English and asked us where we were from. When we told them "San Francisco," they serenaded us with "I left my heart in San Francisco" for the rest of the tram ride, frightening some Austrian skiers in the process! At the top of the mountain Roberto Mastrodicasa left his group and skied with John and me for the next two days. Following the ski trip he invited me to meet his family in Florence. I planned to visit for two days and stayed for more than two weeks. While Roberto and his wife worked, I hopped on Roberto's Vespa and explored Florence and the surrounding countryside. At one o'clock every afternoon, however, I made sure to be back at the Mastrodicasa's. That was when Clara, Roberto's mom, put lunch on the table. Clara loved cooking, and I loved Italian food: We were a perfect match. Thus began a lifelong relationship with the wonderful Mastrodicasa family. I have visited them a dozen times, they have come to the United States, and my parents have been guests in their home.

Gaetano, Roberto's father, once said to me, "My mother spent twenty-four hours making a spaghetti sauce. Clara spends

RAISING THE BAR

THE STORY OF CLIF BAR, INC.

CLARA AND GAETANO MASTRODICASA, FLORENCE, ITALY.
—GARY ERICKSON

twelve hours and my daughter-in-law buys sauce at the store.
I can taste the difference. Something is happening to our culture and the food of our culture. We are so busy." I had watched
Clara and the care she put into her cooking. She made all her
sauces and pastries. She made pasta by hand. Clara and Gaetano would go to the countryside to buy a particular sausage
from a man who made just a few kilos every week. Each day
they walked to the local market for fresh fruit, meats, and
cheese. Preparing meals was a ritual that took hours, and at
night the whole family gathered to talk and eat.

I fell in love with Italy and savored the art of preparing food
and then enjoying it with family and friends. Four years after
my visit, Carlo Petrini founded the International Slow Food
Movement, advocating the use of locally grown foods and
wines, traditional recipes, and eating as a social event. Slow
Food evolved into a global movement that defends vegetable,
animal, and cultural diversity, organic agriculture, and family
farms. It remains rooted, however, in the pleasures of food,
wine, and companionship. The Mastrodicasas lived the slow
food movement. I grew up with slow food as well. My grandmother Kali taught me how to make phylo dough by hand. We
would lay dough over chairs and tables and let it sit for hours.
Now my daughter Lydia and I spend hours making things
from phylo.

Why does someone who appreciates food traditions and slow
food make an energy bar designed for convenience and porta-
bility? The slow food movement promotes indigenous seed pres-
ervation and cultivation, artisan-handcrafted foods, locally

grown ingredients, and caring and careful food preparation. While recognizing that our products aren't slow, we try to get as close to the slow food vision as possible. We select the best and most nutritious whole grains, oats, soy, chocolates, berries, nuts, and fruits to deliver maximum nutrition and taste. Even though we produce a convenience food we hope people will slow down a bit as they eat our bars, knowing that they are putting something into their bodies that is wholesome and good for them.

Clif ingredients resemble slow rather than fast food. Clif Bars are still made by bakers using mixers, ovens, and cooling racks; just a bit more automated than my mom's kitchen where I baked the first bars. Clif Bar supports sustainable agriculture and small farms by purchasing organic ingredients from people we know and trust; we try to visit our suppliers personally.

We want to create a food culture at Clif Bar. Most Wednesdays employees cook and eat pizzas together using organic spring or winter wheat, fresh mozzarella, locally made sausages, fresh tomatoes, and garlic (and these *are* the world's best pizzas). Three years ago my brother Randy said to the Research and Development team, "Let's take a whole year to investigate the subtle tastes of tea." The team bought the world's best teas and every day made a pot of tea and discussed its taste. How does it react on the tongue? What does it feel like, smell like, what sensation does it give? Is it bitter, sweet, flowery? They still drink a lot of tea! The Clif wine-tasting group meets once a month to explore the taste of (and enjoy!) wines. A geographic growing area or a particular varietal is selected and blind-tasted by a group of eight to twelve people. Two people from the group provide food that matches the wine and explain why they think it matches. We have in-house taste testers that actually educate themselves on the differences between Mexican and Persian lime! They know that they need to be able to make sensory evaluations of our products. People from throughout the company—Finance, Research and Development, Operations, Manufacturing, and Brand—all contribute to our collective taste knowledge. Our people's palates become more sensitive to subtle differences and nuances as we explore the world of taste, texture, and the pleasure of enjoying food. This sensitivity translates to better products and flavors.

Years after my first trip to Italy, my homework assignment to Clif Bar was "What three principles or values would you want on a white-road journey?" Rich Boragno, who is Italian, wrote "prosciutto and vino." I asked him what his response meant, and he said that prosciutto and vino symbolize enjoying life and savoring the moment. Carlo Petrini said that when he ate prosciutto he knew it would become part of him, body and soul. It had better be good and he had better enjoy it. As a company we find ways to savor the moment. We believe that great taste, enjoyment of food, and attention to ingredients can come together in a convenient food as well as in a leisurely Italian dinner.

Take a break, enjoy some prosciutto and vino.

RANDY ERICKSON AND RICH BORAGNO IN CLIF KITCHEN.
—KATHY ERICKSON

" The slow food movement fascinates me. It is not just about gastronomy and connection with local sustainable food. It blends the environmental movement's concern about biodiversity with farmers' rights, food justice, food itself, enjoyment of eating, and the connection to family. Clif Bar started because of the enjoyment of eating (or the displeasure at eating someone else's bar).

What do eating at Chez Panisse and eating a Clif Bar have in common? I think the philosophies fit together; there are occasions when each makes sense. A three-hour dinner at Chez Panisse is always a wonderful experience. Eating a Clif Bar should also be a wonderful experience because it is whole grain, nutritious, has great texture, and was created by people who love to eat well. "

—RANDY ERICKSON, VICE PRESIDENT OF INNOVATION

RAISING
THE BAR

THE STORY OF CLIF BAR, INC.

> **LESSON SIX: KNOW NOTHING**

After John returned to the United States I was on my own,
with no plans. I had a plane ticket for India in September and
a ticket back to the United States from Nepal in a year. These
were my only set dates. A few friends promised to join me for
parts of the adventure, but I was on my own most of the time.
First I took a small pack and traveled all over Europe. I slept
in parks and trains in Switzerland and camped in the snow in
Italy. I enjoyed Germany, France, Switzerland, and Austria.
I traveled to Greece, where my grandmother Kali was born,
and gained fifteen pounds!

Traveling through Israel was especially powerful. I had no real
agenda for my visit, didn't understand Middle East politics, and
possessed no strong bias. I flew into Tel Aviv. Descending from
the plane I was surprised to see a soldier on the tarmac holding
a machine gun. Military personnel with machine guns lined
every step as I walked through customs. I came from a country
that had not suffered war on its soil during my lifetime. I wasn't
used to seeing so many men with machine guns. I stayed in
Jerusalem for a week with a Jewish friend of my parents and
engaged her in intense conversations about Israeli politics.
Each day the news reported killings; rock throwing and fighting
were common in the old part of Jerusalem. I could feel the tension in the air.

One evening near Nazareth two young boys approached me
while I was setting up camp in an orchard. They asked me
where I was from and what I was doing. I told them about my
trip, and they opened up. They talked about their family and

JERUSALEM, ISRAEL.
—GARY ERICKSON

RAISING THE BAR

THE STORY OF CLIF BAR, INC.

the history of the area. They told me that the land where I was camping had been taken from their father. Again, politics permeated our discussion. I traveled around Israel for a month and spent most of that month talking with Palestinians and Israelis. I asked many questions and left with few answers.

I next traveled to India and Nepal. I grew up in middle-class America. My family didn't have a lot of money, but all my needs were met, and more. I never had to worry about whether I would eat or not. It sobered me to see people in India and Nepal struggling to meet basic needs. I saw porters carrying 150 pounds day after day to earn two dollars, trashing their feet and bodies in the process. I saw countless people without limbs begging on city sidewalks. I saw malnourished children on every corner.

My trip around the world humbled me. I grew up believing that there were right and wrong ways of doing things, that much of life is black and white. My month in Israel and three months in India and Nepal deeply changed my understanding of the world and life. It was difficult for me to hold on to absolutes. Given the wide variety of peoples, cultures, religions, and beliefs that I encountered, I couldn't help but realize how little I knew. The trip freed me from feeling that I needed to have answers. It taught me to ask questions.

After telling a story from my Nepal trip at a Thursday Morning Meeting, I read Wendell Berry's line, "Ask the questions that have no answers." I knew that I could say, with Pico Iyer, "[the] point of travel for me is to journey into complication, even contradiction: to confront the questions that I never have to think about at home and am not sure can ever be easily answered."

Cultures, including corporate cultures, differ dramatically. Some people may not feel comfortable at Clif Bar, may experience it as foreign. They may enter Clif, see us as a small entrepreneurial company, and want to take us to the red road. Much of what they see at our company may not make sense to them; it may not fit the business world with which they are familiar. I appreciate the experience they bring, but their first task is to learn about our culture, as strange as it may seem to them at first. We recently hired someone with experience in a bigger company. He asked me for advice as he took the job. I told him, "Ask questions more than give answers. Even when you think you have the answer, turn it into a question. You will find that there are ways we do things here that won't make sense to you, and you will want to change it. Figure it out first."

At Clif Bar I try to model the value of knowing nothing—of asking questions, avoiding absolutes, being humble, and seeking the wisdom of others—as a leadership and business style.

➤ LESSON SEVEN: CAUSE AND EFFECT

My friend Sheila joined me for part of my trip to India and Nepal. We had worked together as mountain guides and hoped to trek and climb together in the Himalayas. Her friend Doug joined us for a stretch of the trip. As the three of us headed for Jumla in western Nepal, I developed an intestinal illness. I was all too familiar with the symptoms, since I had previously

RAISING THE BAR

THE STORY OF CLIF BAR, INC.

TREKKING IN THE HIMALAYAS, NEPAL.
—GARY ERICKSON (TOP), SHEILA ILSICIN (BOTTOM)

contracted giardia in the Alps and in the California Sierra. Sheila and Doug graciously offered to wait for me to recover. Knowing that my health might not hold out, I told them to go on without me. I ended up traveling on my own for three weeks, recovering from my intestinal illness. I moved slowly for several days, heading north toward the Annapurna mountain range. At one point, I stopped in a village near the Tibetan border, high in the Himalayas. I still suffered from the intestinal illness and found it difficult to eat. One day, as I sat near a stream gazing up at the mountains, I began to idly watch the Nepalese family to whom I paid $2 a day for room and board. The mother was washing dishes in the stream as the children played. I looked upstream about twenty feet and watched as the young daughter defecated in the stream. I looked back downstream where her mother continued cleaning dishes in the same river water. I was about to eat dinner in this woman's home. I thought, "Well. I know why I'm sick." There was a clear chain of cause and effect between the little girl's action, the mother's dishwashing, and illness (not just mine).

Years later I thought of this story when Elysa, our company ecologist, and I talked about our sustainability initiative. She asked me, "What effect do you think our business has on the environment?" I pictured the little girl and her mother. I wondered, "Do we affect the environment in ways we aren't

RAISING THE BAR

THE STORY OF CLIF BAR, INC.

even aware of?" I asked myself, "How are we soiling the stream?" Now at Clif we seek ways to diminish our impact on the environment.

The Nepali stream story taught me a key lesson: we need to understand cause and effect. The spirit of this story led us to take a hard look at all of our ingredients, how they are grown and how they affect the environment. I want Clif Bar to look at the environmental impact of all we do as a business—from the field to the final product.

> ### LESSON EIGHT: MAKE A MUTANT DESIGN

I was depressed for months after I returned from my 1982 world tour. I parked cars again and tried to figure out what to do with my life. One day my brother Randy asked me if I wanted to work in a factory. Avocet, a bicycle products company, had just bought into the foundry business that he owned. Avocet and Randy planned to make high-end racing components as well as bicycle seats that were actually comfortable. Randy invited me to sweep floors at Avocet's new manufacturing facility. I took him up on the offer, not knowing that I wouldn't be sweeping floors for long. The person hired to run the new facility was fired, leaving my brother Randy (and me) in charge of a near-empty warehouse with a dinosaur-age machine for making bicycle saddles. The company was so behind on bike saddle production that we worked fourteen-to-sixteen-hour days seven days a week for six months to catch up! I knew virtually nothing about engineering when I started. I soon felt as if I'd received a degree in manufacturing and industrial design from Randy. After eight months, Randy returned to his foundry,

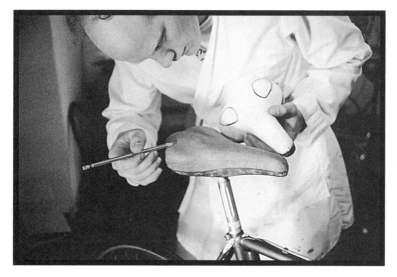

DESIGNING BIKE SEATS. —RANDY ERICKSON

and Avocet asked me to stay on as plant manager of the saddle factory. I went from college to mountain guiding to traveling around the world to parking cars to managing fifty people manufacturing seats. Not your standard career path.

We had full vertical integration, meaning that we made the entire saddle in this factory, except for one piece. We designed the plastic shell, but it was made outside the plant. We did everything else on-site. We had a tool and die maker. We had a machine shop. I learned about bicycle seats and made some interesting discoveries. The anatomy of the part of the body that rests on the bicycle seat differs for men and women! If a woman uses a seat designed for a man, it hurts. We pioneered seats that were specifically designed for women; the idea wasn't rocket science but no one had ever done it.

RAISING
THE BAR

THE STORY OF CLIF BAR, INC.

We wanted to make comfortable seats, which got me interested in alternative materials. I found out about a gel material made by Spenco Gel. This liquidy, gooey material was difficult to get into a bike saddle. I spent countless hours experimenting in the factory. I wasn't an engineer, but I kept asking questions and trying different techniques. Eventually I developed a manufacturing technique that integrated the gel into the saddle. In the mid-1980s, Avocet manufactured the first integrated gel saddle based on my design, and from that point on, gel saddles became synonymous with comfort. During the period I was working at Avocet, computer automated design (CAD) and computer automated manufacturing (CAM) became standard practice for industrial design and manufacturing. For my next designing foray—the O2 saddle—I designed the shape and general artistic look, Marty Holloway did the CAD/CAM engineering and product coding, and Doug Gilmour created the graphics and named the saddle the "O2." In 1995 The Museum of Modern Art in New York featured the O2 saddle as part of the exhibition: "Mutant Materials in Contemporary Design."

It may seem a stretch, but my experience in manufacturing and with Randy helped me at Clif Bar. Baking for me is both art and science. Most energy bars, even our Luna Bars, have defined forms with square edges. I created the die for Clif Bar on a CAD/CAM system because I wanted a bar that didn't have tight little corners. All Clif Bars turn out differently, with a variety of shapes and sizes. Clif Bars have a mutant design. I still believe that one of the folksy and special things about Clif Bars is that they feel handmade. Experimenting with flavors and textures remains central to Clif Bar. At times I nail a recipe within days, but other times it takes weeks to find a flavor that satisfies me. In our test kitchen our research and development team may experiment with products for months before we get what we want.

So if you are ever out on a bike ride, enjoying a Clif Bar, and sitting on an O2 or gel saddle, raise your hat to mutant design!

➤ LESSON NINE: BREAK FROM THE FRONT

I've always considered my decision to race bicycles one of my best decisions. I loved the speed of the bicycle and being on the road. My racing friends introduced me to a new world, a sport that combines teamwork and individual performance. Bike racing strategy is complex; it reminds me of a moving, athletic chess game. At its essence racing possesses a beautiful rhythm. You travel at thirty miles per hour with a bloc of cyclists, the peloton, that may contain one or two hundred riders. You ride inches away from bikes ahead of and behind you. Various dynamics come into play during a race. You can win by sprinting out ahead of the peloton at the end of a race. Or you can join a group of riders who break from the front of the peloton. A breakaway group can include cyclists from different teams, in which case the break begins a race within a race. You can find yourself working with an archrival to make the break succeed, and although a breakaway group takes the lead by working as a team, the individual members are competing against each other at the same time. The first person in a break rides as hard as possible, pulling the rest of the riders along behind. A front person who tires moves back, and someone else takes over. The former

RAISING THE BAR

THE STORY OF CLIF BAR, INC.

TOUR OF MARIN BIKE RACE.
—CLEM DONAHUE

front rider recovers, pulled along by the group. These pushes and pulls may take seconds or minutes. At times riders rotate like highly synchronized clockwork, beautiful to watch.

Clockwork. Rotation. Beauty. Racing also involves mind games and risk. Do you try to get into the break? Can you get in the break? With whom do you want to break? These questions shape the chess game of the ride. If you join a breakaway group and the peloton catches the group, the race is over for you. Fresh riders, who haven't exhausted their energy by breaking away, will certainly beat you. If you risk breaking away, you've taken your shot. In this mental chess game a rider can win races even if not as physically fit as other racers.

The ideal, of course, is to be both smart and fit. Between 1986 and 1990 I won a few races, and I still compete several times a year. I never raced full time or spent 100 percent of my time on training, yet when I was out there riding, I wanted to experience the essence of the sport—to truly race the race, to break away from the peloton. I wanted to take the risk, to try to get into those breaks, to attempt to win races. I found that I suffered more when I stayed in the pack than when I was in front of the peloton or in the breaks, pushing my limits.

The point: Clif Bar started in the break. If an energy bar peloton had existed, then PowerBar was the solo breakaway. Clif Bar decided to take the risk and bridge from the peloton up to PowerBar. Balance Bar joined Clif; we moved up together. Balance Bar and Clif Bar were friendly to each other, glad that we could open up the bar category to new players. Now a whole

RAISING THE BAR

THE STORY OF CLIF BAR, INC.

new wave of bars, similar to a new peloton, chases PowerBar, Balance Bar, and Clif Bar. We look over our shoulders and ask, "Where did you come from?" Trying to break away and leave the pack is the essence of the sport of business. Some people like to feel comfortable owning a business, content to be in the pack, creating good products, making money. This is a fine approach to business, but it isn't ours.

To be in the essence of sport or business you have to be fit. At Clif Bar we want to be in the front break, away from the pack.

➤ A LOVE STORY WITH NO APPARENT BUSINESS POINT

My dear friend Tad had been happily married to Heidi for a few years when we had a conversation about relationships. He asked me, "So, what are you looking for?" "What do you mean, what am I looking for?" I replied. "You know, would you like to get married someday?" he responded. I said, "Well, it doesn't seem to be happening for me." There were moments during my twenties and thirties when I wondered if I would ever get married, but I was happy and took a *que sera, sera* attitude. He then asked me, "Well, what would do it for you? What are you looking for in a partner?" My instant reply was "Well, Kit would work."

KIT AND GARY. —CLAYTON WARD

I first met Kit in 1978 through her best friend Elysa (who is now our company ecologist). I felt an instant "something" but tried to ignore it since she had a boyfriend. Instead, we developed a friendship. Two years later I roomed with Tad for six months while studying at a post-college liberal arts program in Oregon. Tad knew about my crush on Kit and that I wasn't pursuing her because she was engaged. That fall Kit, Elysa, and I spent a climbing weekend in Yosemite Valley, and I became even more infatuated. She was cute, a dancer, very alive, and now I found out that she climbed, performing ballet on rock. I was beside myself but again respected Kit's engagement. We continued our friendship, and in 1982 I left for my round-the-world trip.

Halfway through my trip Elysa wrote to me from a pub in Noe Valley, San Francisco, updating me on our mutual Sierra Treks friends. Then she wrote, "Kit just walked in and told me she broke up with her fiancé. I am so happy. I didn't think they were good together." Here I was halfway around the world, hitchhiking in Switzerland, and Kit was free for the first time in the four years I had known (and been infatuated) with her. I waited a few days and wrote a letter I never sent. What I wanted to say, but didn't, was, "I'll be in San Francisco in six months. Can you wait until I get back? I would like to take you to dinner." I chickened out, and when I returned Kit had a new boyfriend and was soon married. We continued our friendship. I respected her marriage, and for fourteen years I never revealed my feelings to her. She had no idea.

Kit called near the end of Clif's first year in 1992. She said, "My husband and I have split up." Earlier I had invited Kit, her husband, and their children to a cabin I rented in Hope Valley, south of Lake Tahoe. She went on, "Can I take you up on that offer to go to your cabin? My kids and I need to get away." I said, "Of course." She suggested a date and I realized that I would be up there as well. I said, "Look, I'll be up there but there are a lot of rooms for you and the children. Come on up." I immediately called my friends Tad and George for advice. The clear consensus was to say nothing, do nothing: Let her get past this rough spot and see what happens down the road. The first evening we stayed up talking after she put the children to bed. To my surprise, she revealed that now that she wasn't married she was interested in romance. With me! Here we were making this discovery about each other fourteen years after we first met. Rest assured that we didn't pass each other up this time. It felt completely right and still does. It was worth the wait.

Actually there is a business point to this love story. Without a partner who believes in you and shares your vision, you may feel alone on the white-road journey. As you can tell from reading this book, Kit's presence and values permeate the company and its vision. I'm fortunate to ride with a great partner, in business and in love.

RAISING THE BAR

THE STORY OF CLIF BAR, INC.

CHAPTER 6

SOLO CLIMBING

(MAINTAINING CONTROL FOR THE LONG HAUL)

I may not be a world-class mountain climber, but I've enjoyed numerous adventures on peaks around the world. I've scaled the face of Half Dome in Yosemite Valley; slept two nights in Mount Rainier's crater; ascended Monte Rosa (the highest mountain in Switzerland) and Mount Hood in Oregon. I've even climbed solo. My friends and I climb alpine style: we move quickly, carry light packs, take along few people. I've been to the Himalayas in Nepal, but after an experience there, I've never been interested in traditional big-time climbing expeditions.

> ALPINE VERSUS EXPEDITIONARY CLIMBING

While trekking in Nepal, I met up with an expedition about to climb Dhaligiri, one of the world's highest peaks. For days I played cat and mouse with the group, carefully observing its climbing style. I counted more than two hundred porters carrying satellite dishes, solar panels, skis, oxygen bottles, and lots of food. I figured that if each porter carried a hundred pounds,

ON SUMMIT OF MONTE ROSA, ITALY/SWITZERLAND. —JULIE CHRISTINSON

CLIMBING IN CHAMONIX, FRANCE.
—JULIE CHRISTINSON

RAISING THE BAR

THE STORY OF CLIF BAR, INC.

the expedition must have been traveling with at least twenty thousand pounds of stuff; all of this to get about six people to the top of the peak (if they were lucky). Seeing the Dhaligiri expedition, and others like it, convinced me that I never wanted to climb Mount Everest or similar peaks using this method. Expeditions that require hundreds of porters, a dozen Sherpas, and tons of equipment just don't appeal to me.

Traditional expeditionary or "siege" climbing is methodical. First you set up base camp. Next, some climbers set up Camp 2 while others move ahead to work on Camp 3. Climbers, Sherpas, and porters travel back and forth between camps ferrying loads of supplies. To me it seems tedious and predictable. Sure, you might encounter bad weather, avalanches, crevasses, and rock falls to make life more exciting, but the travel in and of itself is slow and monotonous.

One of the characteristics of expedition climbing that bothers me the most is the garbage left in its wake. I'm talking about real garbage. People who consider themselves environmentalists climb in some of the world's most beautiful spots—Mount Everest, K2, Denali—and leave behind tons (literally) of garbage. I've seen base and high-altitude camps littered with hundreds of oxygen bottles, deserted tents, climbing equipment, food, and garbage. Fifty tons of nonbiodegradable trash

PORTERS HEADING TO
DHALIGIRI, NEPAL.
—GARY ERICKSON

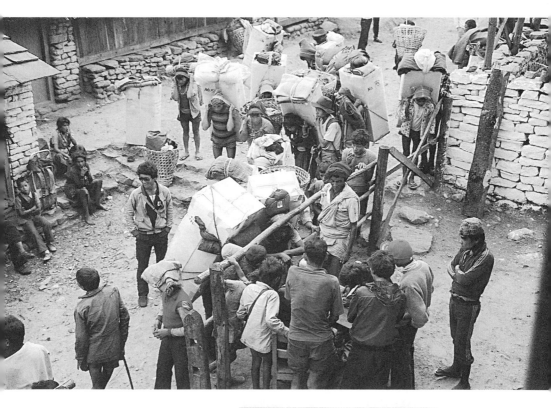

TRASH AT SHYANGBOCHE FROM EVEREST BASE CAMP.
—LIESL CLARK

"I'm talking about real garbage . . ."

everest **TRASHed**

"I've seen base and high-altitude camps
littered with hundreds of oxygen bottles . . .

Fifty tons of
nonbiodegradable trash
has been left
on Mt. Everest since
the **1950s** and it's left up

to concerned volunteers to remove it."

have been left on Mt. Everest since the 1950s and it's left up to concerned volunteers to remove it. Does a few people's obsession with getting to the top justify trashing beautiful mountains?

Alpine-style climbing differs radically from such high-impact expeditionary mountaineering. In alpine climbing, since you're climbing with limited supplies, you must move fast; you can't carry any excess. On our climbs, my buddies and I carried everything on our backs; we were self-sufficient. When Bruce and I climbed Half Dome we lugged enough water for the entire three-day climb on our backs from the Yosemite Valley floor to the base of Half Dome. On the climb we hauled the water, our food, climbing equipment, clothes, and sleeping gear up a vertical rock wall. In alpine-style climbing you may not climb the highest peaks in the world, but you get to climb on your own, unencumbered by a mountain of stuff.

In the end, what bothers me about expeditionary climbing is how much energy, equipment, money, and people it takes to put a handful of individuals on top of a mountain. The obsession to reach the top reminds me of the red-road mentality: it doesn't matter how you get there, just that you reach your destination. Alpine-style climbers are more likely to have a white-road mentality and a low-impact environmental ethos. I have never left anything behind on a mountain, whether it was food, climbing equipment, or a Clif Bar wrapper. Our campsites on beautiful mountains are destinations; they aren't a means to an end.

I guess I don't believe in reaching the top at any cost.

Clif Bar's journey resembles alpine climbing, rather than a high-impact expedition to the top of Everest. As the owners of Clif Bar Inc., Kit and I hold shareholder values that commit us to keeping the company and the earth healthy. We don't draw every penny out of the company. We try to travel light and to leave little garbage behind. We have the privilege of continuing to create a company that expresses our deepest values. Many of our decisions would make no sense if we owned a company that was revenue-driven and climbing just to be sold—the business equivalent of an expedition to Mount Everest.

➤ HOW TO LOSE YOUR COMPANY WITHOUT REALLY TRYING—OWNERSHIP OPTIONS

Clif Bar was a fifty-fifty partnership for fourteen years. After the partnership ended, I had the opportunity to change the structure of Clif Bar Inc. through various ownership options: taking on venture capital, merging with a public company, selling to a larger company, allowing a big company to purchase a small stake in Clif Bar, asking family and friends to invest, and going public. In the end, I decided that 100 percent private ownership, the business equivalent of low-impact alpine climbing, was the best option if I wanted to embrace the vision I describe in this book.

Fifty-Fifty Ownership

In 1985 while eating Yohas with my mom I thought, "Gosh. I could start a business with these things." My Greek grandmother Kalliope, who inspired my entire family, taught my mom how

RAISING
THE BAR

THE STORY OF CLIF BAR, INC.

to make the beautiful, delicious Greek pastry. My mom adapted the recipe, creating Yohas with brioche dough and concocting fillings like spinach and feta, meat, and pesto-zucchini. They were tasty! A year later, I started Kali's Sweets and Savories (named after my grandmother). Many delis in the San Francisco Bay Area were already selling prepared foods, such as knishes and empanadas, to add variety to their traditional sandwich-and-salad menus. At Kali's, we baked and sold Yohas and gourmet cookies wholesale to delis and other outlets.

I asked my friend Lisa to join me in getting Kali's off the ground. We started the bakery with $1,000 from my personal savings (used to buy a mixer), and I threw in a few hundred dollars a month to fund Kali's initial growth. You wouldn't call us overcapitalized! Although I was sole owner, I promised Lisa future profit sharing. There came a time when the stress of running Kali's while holding down another full-time job became too much for me, and I wanted to close the business. Instead Lisa proposed that she run operations in exchange for 50 percent of the company. That way I could decrease my day-to-day involvement. At that point we were in the red and boasted whopping annual sales of $20,000. Fifty percent of zero annual profits is zero, so Lisa's idea didn't seem at all unreasonable! Lisa had contributed serious sweat equity during Kali's early years. I was glad to have a partner and thought, "We are going to do this together." A fifty-fifty partnership seemed the right thing to do, and I believed it could work for the long haul.

The allure of fifty-fifty ownership is understandable. I've talked to many entrepreneurs and visionaries who pursued equal partnerships because they wanted someone to share the path with them. They believed that because both partners possessed equal shares, both would give everything to the business; they would have the same amount of skin in the game. Equal sharing is compelling on many levels.

My attorney, Bruce Lymburn, claims that most fifty-fifty partnerships face a day of reckoning. It comes when partners no longer share a common vision for the company. The core problem is that neither person holds ultimate control. If you don't agree on critical issues you may reach a stalemate and compromise decisions and directions in the process. What happens if one partner wants to exit? Or doesn't want to work anymore? Or wants to move the company in a completely new direction? A company gets polarized if partners differ in their visions. Today, I don't believe that two equal heads are better than one.

Yvon Chouinard started Chouinard Equipment, a climbing hardware business, with a partner. Yvon became interested in clothing and wanted to start Patagonia as a separate company. Yvon

RAISING **THE BAR**

THE STORY OF CLIF BAR, INC.

and his partner had shared similar visions up to that point, but the partner wasn't interested in a clothing company, and Yvon eventually bought his half. Ken Grossman of Sierra Nevada Brewery faced a similar situation. Ken's partner was no longer interested in growing the company, and in order to maximize his equity his legal advisers wanted the company to go public, merge with another company, or sell. Ken wanted to remain private, and he ended up buying out his partner. Currently both Yvon and Ken are 100 percent owners of their companies. Many people begin with fifty-fifty partnerships and end up trying to buy out their partners, often at great cost. I now believe that it's unrealistic to expect that a business partnership will last forever.

A day of reckoning finally came for Lisa and me—and Clif Bar. When we'd struck up the partnership, I didn't have legal advice. I hadn't understood the implications of giving away 50 percent of the company, although people had warned me that I should keep control of at least 51 percent of the company since the original vision, capital outlay, and recipes were mine. Although entrepreneurs told me sweat equity merited 10–20 percent of the company, I innocently thought it was worth 50 percent. Little did I know that a 50 percent owner would have the power to dissolve the company, which was the threat I was given by Lisa. So, fourteen years later, when my partner wanted to exit, I needed a Plan B: I needed a new ownership option, fast.

Selling the Company

In many ways, selling involves fewer headaches than other options. Some entrepreneurs start a company with an exit strategy of selling in mind. Selling a company in a cash deal, as we almost did, is the cleanest way to exit, but if you choose to sell, you've got to be able to truly let go of your company. I've seen many people who plan to run their companies after the sale, only to realize that they can't be the primary guiding force any longer. I have seen others suffer depression following the sale of their businesses, even if they made clean exits. My friend Jim Gentes founded Gyro, a company that produced great, safe bicycle helmets. In spite of Gyro's excellent reputation, Jim faced numerous legal battles due to liability issues in the helmet industry, and he sold the company. Jim told me that it took him three years to feel really good following the sale, even though he knew it was time for him to sell. Another friend, Tom Ritchey, sold 80 percent of Ritchey (maker of bicycles and components) to Specialized. He was so unhappy after the sale that he ended up buying the company back. He now owns Ritchey 100 percent.

WHY DO PEOPLE SELL THEIR COMPANIES? One of the top reasons is burnout. Creating and running a business is hard work and extremely stressful. It's a 24/7 job that holds the owner ultimately responsible for everything in the company, from A to Z. Few people understand that burden. The temptation to sell, to rest and rejuvenate, can be strong. If you sell, though, you may ask yourself later, "Could I have recuperated and dealt with the stress in another way?"

Security is another reason owners sell. Although you don't know what will happen from year to year, you wonder if your company will still be around thirty years from now. You wonder if you'll ever have enough of a financial cushion so that you can stop worrying about your long-term financial security. If you sell, money worries go away, which certainly makes it appealing.

RAISING THE BAR

THE STORY OF CLIF BAR, INC.

Another issue in play is fear of competition. When Clif Bar started we competed with a handful of bars; now literally hundreds of bars fill the market. That level of competition can overwhelm you and selling is an understandable response.

A small company may need capital and pursue alternative ownership options. If you are like me, someone who doesn't want to share control of the company, you may prefer to sell rather than face that situation. You may feel that your company has grown beyond your ability to run it. In my case, I thought Clif Bar might grow to become a company with $1 million in sales. How do you go from thinking you can run a $1 million company to managing a $100 million business? A company may just grow too big for its owner. Another owner might sell because the ship is going down, forcing a sale before the company fails. Or maybe you want to spend more time with your children, travel, write checks to favorite causes, or help the world in another way. Certainly there is nothing wrong with selling for these positive reasons.

I believe, however, that many people sell because they think they have to.

If you are concerned with the integrity of your brands and the welfare of your people, selling can break your heart. You have to live with what others do with the company you created. You have to watch as valued employees are laid off. Many consumers won't know that you sold the company and wonder why you are now making decisions that betray company values. You have to live with the what-ifs. I know that if I had sold Clif Bar I would have spent the rest of my life asking, "What if I had kept the company? Could we have made it?"

Venture Capital

Venture capital is a great term. It implies adventure! Venture capitalists take risks by funding start-up companies and individuals with ideas but no money. They demand a high return on investment, generally 35–40 percent compounded annually. Venture capitalists justify this high return on investment because the success rate of new companies is so low: Only three or four out of ten succeed. The founder receives capital but surrenders control from the very beginning of the deal; a venture capital firm will want controlling interest in the company as well as an exit strategy. If you can't exit by paying them off, the company will either be sold or go public.

I entertained the venture capital route. As I described in Chapter Three, originally my partner talked about $25 million up front and the remainder paid over the next five years. Since I

RAISING THE BAR

THE STORY OF CLIF BAR, INC.

couldn't get a large enough loan, I looked to a group of venture capitalists to bridge the difference. I found that for a mere $12 million, the venture capital group would control 30 percent of Clif Bar. I risked having to sell the company if I couldn't pay back the $50 million demanded by the venture capital group, and essentially I would lose control of the company. Their demands upset me because we weren't some risky start-up. We had a proven track record of profitability and had seen annual sales grow from $700,000 in 1992 to $60 million by the time of the deal. Although it seemed unfair that the venture capitalists would require a 35 percent return on investment and take 30 percent of the company, given my volatile situation and need for money, I considered the deal. When I realized what this option would cost me I decided I couldn't do it.

PowerBar discovered the high cost of this ownership option when it partnered with the venture capital group Hellman & Freeman. Hellman & Freeman took about a 15 percent stake in PowerBar at a venture capital rate of (most likely) 35–40 percent return on investment compounded annually. PowerBar and Hellman & Freeman's intention was to grow PowerBar and go public so that owner Brian Maxwell could continue running the company as the majority shareholder. To make this happen, the company needed to hit the right numbers quarter after quarter, but PowerBar didn't make the requisite return even with an infusion of $20 million. The clock ticked and Hellman & Freeman wanted its money back. PowerBar found itself on the market (never its intention) and was eventually purchased by Nestlé. The owner lost control of the business he founded, along with the dream of running a public company.

Mother Teresa ended up being right when she advised Mo Siegel (as I mentioned in Chapter One). Mo left Celestial Seasonings after selling to Kraft Foods and worked with nonprofit organizations. He told me that he soon realized nonprofit work was his avocation, not vocation. He bought Celestial Seasonings back from Kraft Foods (it hadn't been profitable enough for them). The problem was, to get it back he needed to use venture capital, which leveraged the company so much that he never regained control. The company went public in order to pay the venture capital investment, which led to another sale of Celestial Seasonings to Hain. Mo again is no longer part of the company he founded.

Going Public

When I was searching for a way to keep the company, going public was the least attractive option to me. I had watched as many companies that I admired went public. Ben & Jerry's and Odwalla went public, and I thought it was kind of cool at first. Now we all had an opportunity to share in their success and support values we admired. I have since talked to the founders of both companies and see it differently now. Greg Steltenpohl explained why Odwalla's founders decided to go public at a Spirit in Business conference I attended. According to Greg, Odwalla needed capital to buy equipment to produce its juices and to grow the company. Its owners went public to gain additional funding, and down the road the company was sold to Coca-Cola. I asked Greg if he wished it had turned out differently. He said, "Absolutely. I just didn't see how we could do it at the time without bringing in capital."

Ben & Jerry's is probably the most famous example of how going public can backfire and betray the owners' intentions and values. Ben Cohen and Jerry Greenfield's belief, as described in their book *Double-Dip,* was that "the best way to make Ben & Jerry's a force for progressive social change was to grow bigger so we could make more profits and give more money away." Going public meant making more money, which meant doing more good in the world. At some point after going public, business at Ben & Jerry's leveled off. Unilever, a large multinational company, offered a share price that institutional shareholders couldn't refuse, and the company was sold. Ben and Jerry no longer control their company. I met Ben Cohen at a hotel in San Francisco to talk to him about my dilemma—I needed advice. I greatly admired Ben as someone who pioneered socially responsible business practices in the food industry and felt honored that he would take the time to speak with me. He encouraged me to stay the course and do whatever I could to keep Clif Bar private and maintain control of the company.

Friends from Balance Bar told me that they became slaves to Wall Street after going public: They had to worry constantly about share prices. The controlling owner eventually decided to sell Balance Bar to Kraft. These stories demonstrate that when companies Clif's size go public, increasing profits for shareholders becomes the new driving force, and the companies often end up sold. Or, if companies can't perform to Wall Street standards, share prices drop so low that they are de-listed, as happened in the case of Garden Burger.

I didn't want to become a slave to Wall Street—I'm an entrepreneur who cherishes freedom. I can't say that it is never right to go public. I can say, if you don't have to, don't do it.

Minority Shareholder

The minority shareholder option seems attractive at first glance. In this alternative a large company buys a small part of another company. Advantages to this option include marketing muscle provided by the larger company; increased purchasing power of ingredients; greater media access; marketing, infrastructure, corporate, and management power; and capital to grow. Shortly after I turned down the venture capital firm, Cadbury Schweppes called me. They were interested in Clif Bar because the confectionary market in Europe had flattened. Clif Bar Inc. and the growth of the nutrition category in the United States intrigued them. They asked if they could visit for an informal talk about a possible strategic alliance or joint venture. We spent a day together in the summer of 2000 exploring the potential for working together. I was pretty desperate for money to pay off my debt to Lisa, but, by now, I also knew the

RAISING THE BAR

THE STORY OF CLIF BAR, INC.

problems with exit strategies. I put my stake in the ground and said, "I know what typically happens in these situations. You will want an exit strategy, and I'm not going to give it to you. You'll want a certain amount of control over Clif Bar Inc., and I won't give it to you." I had been down this road before with both Mars Inc. and the venture capital firm and didn't want to travel it again. I was willing to give Cadbury Schweppes a say in product launches and budget, a vote on a board, but not an exit strategy. They seemed open to alternative approaches, but in the end they couldn't accept the deal without an exit strategy.

All the big companies I talked to while looking for a minority shareholder wanted an exit strategy. Most wanted to grow Clif Bar Inc. and then, within five years, either buy the company or be bought out. I have yet to hear of a similar situation where the bigger company didn't require an exit strategy. It makes sense that a company a hundred times our size would want the right to buy us out. Exit strategies, however, are the kiss of death if you want to sustain your company and its vision. A new minority partner often takes a large role in decision making and may require 100 percent consensus on salaries, annual budgets, product introductions, style of advertising, and so on. In nearly all cases, the minority shareholder demands more power than its actual investment warrants.

If a minority shareholder hopes to buy a company or be bought out within five years, then why not just sell immediately? The answer is easy: Money. If your company's current revenue is $10 million, you can go to market and sell it for possibly double the revenues, or $20 million. Say Company "T" invests $2 million and becomes a 20 percent stakeholder. If Company "T," through its marketing muscle, brings your company to $50 million, you can now sell for $100 million and walk away with $80 million. (Company "T" gets $20 million, or ten times its investment!) You put up with the headache, loss of control, and inability to express your values through your company so that you can exit with an enormous pocketful of cash.

I'm hoping that a few brave souls can prove the exception to the rule on minority shareholders. In an interview with *Mother Jones,* Gary Hirschberg of Stonyfield Farms said of his deal with Groupe Danone, "There's no doubt I had to choose which devil to dance with." Hirschberg hopes that the increased market share and purchasing power offered by Groupe Danone (the large France-based corporation that bought 40 percent of Stonyfield Farms) will help him pursue his dream of saving New England dairy farms and promoting organic milk. It makes me nervous, however, that Groupe Danone will only retain Hirshberg as CEO if Stonyfield continues to produce double-digit growth. I hope that Hirschberg pulls it off.

Family and Friends

I also looked into getting friends and family to invest in the company. Some companies prefer this because it feels truer to the original, homegrown spirit of a privately held company. But I didn't need to spend a whole lot of time analyzing this option. My dad worked for the state, my mom was a retired schoolteacher, one brother was an artist, and the other worked for

CLIMBING WASHINGTON COLUMN.
—BRUCE HENDRICKS

Clif Bar. I went through my list of friends: They were teachers, social workers, artists, dancers, mountain climbers, cyclists, and medical students. Between all of them they might not be able to take me out to dinner, much less loan me money to pay off the debt! Not a crowd with a lot of spare cash to invest. I consider my friends to be the richest people in the world, but it certainly isn't because of their material possessions and financial wealth. When I told my friends the amount of money I needed, I sounded like a being from another planet. My brother-in-law worked with homeless people who were trying to find a buck, and here I was talking to him about millions of dollars. It was surreal.

Another friend (who actually had an income and connections) said she could ask a few friends to invest in the company. It made me nervous. Even with friends, or in this case friends of friends, the issue of an exit strategy looms large. What happens when some people want to sell their shares? Gary Hirschberg's friends and family (some 297 of them!) invested in Stonyfield Farms. When some investors needed their money out, the company couldn't pay. To pay these investors, Hirschberg sold 40 percent of the company to Groupe Danone. In 2004 Groupe Danone purchased another 40 percent of the company. The France-based conglomerate will most likely own the entire company—remember the exit strategy?

➤ FIRST ASCENTS: THE ENTREPRENEUR'S ROUTE

First ascents are truly the most adventurous climbs. A first ascent is a climb that no one has attempted before (to your knowledge). You're literally the first person up a rock wall, and it is exhilarating! There's no guidebook. You can't check your route; you can't predict what the climb will be like. You can prepare by analyzing topographical maps, studying the route through binoculars, and taking pictures. But once you're on the rock, you can't even predict what the route will be like a few hundred feet in front of you. First ascents are grand experiments; no matter how skilled you are, you don't know if the route will go. Entrepreneurship reminds me of first-ascent climbing. Clif Bar is my business (and life) equivalent of a first ascent in mountaineering; an ongoing grand experiment.

I think I've always had entrepreneurial tendencies. Like a lot of kids, I had a paper route and a lawn-mowing business. But I developed my own profit-and-loss statement, detailing everything: this much money to buy gas for the mower, this much time and money to sharpen the blades and keep the lawnmower in shape. Even as a kid, I wanted to control my own destiny and buy a few things in the process (like a little black-and-white television). When my brothers and I were adolescents, my dad used to take us skiing, but we had to buy our equipment. So, at the age of fourteen, I went to Alameda Sporting Goods (now Tri-City Sporting Goods) and asked the owner for a job (while drooling over the skis!). He hired me, and I made $1.45 an hour plus a discount on skis. Adolescent heaven! Eventually I attended Ohlone Junior College, and later California Polytechnic at San Luis Obispo where I majored in business. I dreamed of owning a ski shop. My entrepreneurial tendencies also showed up while I was working as a wilderness guide. I became known as the "back-country chef." I experimented with recipes on a little one-burner mountaineer stove, honing my cooking skills. I also dreamed of owning a café or a restaurant some day.

I always struggled with formal education. I had never read a book from cover to cover until 1980, when I attended a post-college liberal arts program in Oregon with my friend Tad. That fall I struggled through Fyodor Dostoevsky's *Brothers Karamozov*—it took me months to finish it. I always figured that I had trouble reading books because I wasn't working hard enough or that I couldn't focus. But then I found out that I had dyslexia and realized that my reading problems weren't due to lack of effort on my part. Recently I read (I enjoy books now) that many entrepreneurs and CEOs struggle with learning disabilities and dyslexia just like I do—Richard Branson, Charles Schwab, and Jay Leno among them. I realized that my learning difficulties didn't have to hold me back from being an entrepreneur or from being successful (as I define success).

Entrepreneurialism is more about a spirit, passion, desire, and way of being than about innate gifts and abilities. It is the willingness to tackle first ascents—climbing new routes.

> ### HOW TO SAVE YOUR COMPANY—STAYING PRIVATE AND KEEPING 100 PERCENT OWNERSHIP

I'm a first-ascent entrepreneur, and I wanted an option that would allow me to guide the direction and vision of the company. I seriously explored all the ownership options described in this chapter. In the end I realized that none of them would work for

RAISING
THE BAR

THE STORY OF CLIF BAR, INC.

me. I now believe, given my own experience and after observing the innocent mistakes made by the owners of companies that I greatly admired, that 100 percent private ownership is the best (and possibly only) way to obtain the redefinition of shareholder value that I describe in this book. *I realize that I may have to fight to keep Clif private for the rest of my life.*

Many people want to invest in socially responsible companies. I understand why they want their values to be expressed through their investments, and I admire them. Yet everyone wants a *financial* return on investment. Shareholder value and return on investment are not just about the money for Kit and me. Since corporations are owned by tens of thousands of faceless shareholders, individuals rarely influence corporate policies and values. It is difficult to get shareholders, whether they comprise 49 percent, 30 percent, or 20 percent of a company, to go along on a white-road journey. I realized that I wouldn't be satisfied with anything less than 100 percent ownership. This might sound greedy, selfish, or like I'm a control freak. And in a sense, I am a control freak (although hopefully not greedy and selfish). It's just that I came to see that 100 percent ownership was the cleanest way to keep the vision alive, to stay on the white road, to make sure the business wasn't just about the money.

There are few models for what we are trying to do at Clif Bar. By the time they reach our size, many companies are no longer private. White Wave, which makes the soy milk Silk, and Horizon, producer of organic dairy products, were sold to Dean Foods, the world's largest dairy company. Hain purchased

Imagine food, another privately held company of our approximate size. Kraft (a subsidiary of Philip Morris) purchased Boca Burger; Quaker Oats (a subsidiary of PepsiCo) bought Mother's Natural Foods; ConAgra acquired Lightlife (maker of tofu dogs). The list goes on and on. Clif Bar Inc. is the only player among the top twenty energy bar companies that has stayed private and independent.

Since Kit and I had no models in the food industry for long-term private ownership, we felt like we were climbing without a guidebook. One hundred percent ownership is unencumbered like an alpine climb and adventurous like a first ascent (the entrepreneur's path). We are on the business equivalent of a first ascent. We can climb without needing to chase quarterly earnings, raise outside capital, or prepare our company for sale. Kit and I control our vision and direction and redefine shareholder value to include more than the bottom line. We have the luxury, with 100 percent ownership, to say that we will accept a lower financial return in order to keep money in the company and shape the kind of company that I describe in the next chapter. Clif wants to be around for the long haul, with values intact. Kit and I, as sole owners, are creating a model for the long term that we believe is rich, in the full sense of the word.

➤ HOW TO KEEP YOUR COMPANY—SUCCESSION, OR DON'T KILL THE ESTATE PLANNERS

Anyone who owns over 50 percent of a company will have to deal with ownership and management succession. Planning for succession is one of the most difficult things faced by entrepreneurs.

RAISING
THE
BAR

THE STORY OF CLIF BAR, INC.

Whether you plan for it or not, your company will be succeeded by someone or something. Who is going to control Clif Bar when Kit and I are no longer here?

Start planning for your succession as soon as you can. You must continually work on your living trust and estate plans, and prepare for catastrophic events that might leave your successors with heavy tax burdens. A debt-free company worth $200 million upon the death of its owners immediately goes into a trust and may owe $100 million in taxes. How does a company come up with $100 million? Unless a good succession plan exists, the company will be sold. If it is just about the money, that outcome doesn't pose a problem—the trust sells the company and pays the taxes. However, if you want to sustain a company, its employees, and its values for the long haul, a good succession plan is critical. Succession and estate planning is a never-ending process; as the company grows so does the plan. It amazes me how few people work on this. I have talked to people who own $700 million companies and have no estate plan.

My advice is simple: No matter how big your company, get counsel and an estate plan as quickly as you can. Take responsibility for the enormous gift that you hope to pass on to the next generation; it's part of the entrepreneur's job.

What about management succession? My aspiration is to own Clif Bar through the course of my life. When you read this book, however, I may not be the CEO of Clif Bar Inc. All CEOs need to think about who will succeed them in running the daily operations of their business. Finding a person or persons who can succeed you is central to a sustainable model.

Patagonia's model fits where I would like to end up. Years ago I sat with Yvon and Malinda Chouinard at climber Ron Kauk's home in Yosemite after a day of rock climbing. I asked about business succession since I knew Yvon no longer ran day-to-day operations at Patagonia. I was impressed that the spirit still seemed so alive in the company. Yvon told me that it took him years and a few tries to find just the right person to serve as Patagonia's CEO. In the early Clif Bar days, Lisa and I wore every hat; we ran day-to-day operations and provided the company vision. I now believe that everything shouldn't depend on the presence and personality of the original founder or entrepreneur. In Chapter Seven I describe how our organizational structure carries the Clif vision in its day-to-day operations.

A company must move from being entrepreneur-centric to being vision-centric.

CHAPTER 7

SUSTAINING OUR LIVING COMPANY

(FIVE ASPIRATIONS BUSINESS MODEL)

What return on investment do I get from a white-road journey or a first ascent? For me, riding and climbing have always been about the whole journey: I love the dreaming, planning, organizing; I love the equipment, the road trip to the mountain, the camping and hiking. I even love cooking food on a rock ledge. My return on investment could be a sunset halfway up a mountain, or finding a cool crack to climb, or pushing myself physically and mentally, or laughing with a buddy. In the same way, I love all aspects of our business: the ideas, the planning, the opportunities to do good in the world; I love creating and manufacturing products, poring over budgets, competing with other brands, working with great people.

Since Kit and I have invested our lives, money, and time in the company, the return on investment had better be worth it. The business world offers just one definition of how to get a worthwhile return on investment: "Maximize shareholder value," the

RAISING
THE
BAR

THE STORY OF CLIF BAR, INC.

old bottom line. Kit and I spent countless hours talking about what we wanted in return for the time, money, and emotion that we invested. We asked ourselves what would make us proud at the end of each year. We knew it wasn't all about the money for us. We knew that we wanted Clif Bar to be healthy over the long haul and that we wanted to keep our company on a white-road journey. As we talked, the term *sustainability* came up again and again. Didn't we want to sustain our brands so we could support our environmental program? Didn't we want to sustain a profit so we could treat our people with the same respect and attentiveness that Clif had over the years? After looking at all we did as a company, we realized that our return on investment boiled down to five aspirations: sustaining our brands, our business, our people, our community, and our planet.

Arie de Geus writes in *The Living Company* that Western corporations have an average life span of approximately thirty

SUSTAINING OUR BRANDS

SUSTAINING OUR BUSINESS

SUSTAINING OUR PEOPLE

SUSTAINING OUR COMMUNITY

SUSTAINING THE PLANET

RAISING
THE
BAR

THE STORY OF CLIF BAR, INC.

OUR BUSINESS ASPIRATIONS

A BALANCED ECOSYSTEM
FOR A THRIVING BUSINESS

to forty years. I want Clif Bar to enjoy a life that is longer and healthier than the norm. I ended Chapter Six by writing that companies need to move from being entrepreneur-centric to vision-centric if they are to thrive over the long haul. In 2002, we formalized the Clif Bar vision into a business model based on our five aspirations. I believe our business model has legs: Other people and companies can adopt (and adapt) this vision-centric model. It is a living grand experiment.

At the end of each year we look carefully at how well we guarded the well-being of our brands, business, people, community, and planet. Each aspiration represents a facet of our return on investment.

➤ FIRST ASPIRATION:
SUSTAINING OUR BRANDS—KEEPING OUR MOJO

The bar began it all. We created a product by responding to an unfulfilled natural demand. We tapped into this natural demand and experienced authentic, organic growth. The brand grew at its own natural pace, but faster than we expected. Now that the brand is more than ten years old, how do we keep it relevant, authentic, and thriving? All companies want to sustain their brands, and we do too, *but* we want to sustain our brand in a way that keeps our unique Clif spirit going!

Natural Demand

I originally thought of Clif Bar as an energy bar for cyclists and climbers—a reasonable view, since it emerged from my own avocations. As it turns out (happily enough), many folks other than sports enthusiasts love Clif Bar. However, we continue to

SUSTAINING OUR BRANDS

KEEPING OUR MOJO

May our brands be around for future generations to tell the story of where we started and what we've become. We are brand parents who obsess over how our brand embryos are formed, how we birth our brands, how we nourish them as they grow, and how we care for them as they mature. We listen acutely to consumers and tap natural demand.

We want to create products that nourish and sustain, whose taste leaves people wanting more, whose quality is never compromised, and whose ingredients tread lightly on the earth.

ALWAYS - ATTENTIVE, ADAPTIVE, ACTIVE

*All facts and information subject to improve.

Nutrition Facts*
Yearly Compilation of Activities

Activity   1yr. Difference

Activity	1yr. Difference
ACV Increase	10%
POP Placements	23,500
Quality Assurance	99%
R&D Explorations	10^3
Events Sponsored	>1000
Athletes Sponsored	1000
Web Hits	>150,000

INGREDIENTS

LunaFest, Luna Chix, Ambassadors, CIA, consumer service, dedications, The Breast Cancer Fund, athletic sponsorships, USPS Cycling Team, Beyond the Podium, Clif Cross Team, seasonal flavors, new flavors, MOJO Bar, key events (Escape from Alcatraz, Sea Otter, Marine Corps. Marathon, Chicago Marathon...etc.), direct mail, merchandisers, strategic promotions, collateral, free samples, quality assurance program, in-house R&D, field reps, direct and broker sales.

maintain close contact with athletes. Our company employs many in-house hard-core athletes, we support more than a thousand amateur-to-world-class athletes, and we meet up with lots more competitors at the thousand-plus events that we attend. This close contact allows us to intimately understand what these consumers desire. We ask them, "What do you want when you are out there competing? What can we create for you that you can't find in the market?" Athletes come to us with their own ideas for product, packaging, flavors, and causes. Athletes told us, for example, that they wanted a natural, good tasting alternative to the gels on the market. We gave them Clif Shot. The germ of another idea came when someone at an outdoor show asked me if I could make a salty potato Clif Bar; they were tired of sweets and wanted salty food in the backcountry. Thus, Mojo Bar was born. Luna Bar came from listening to women who wanted a nutrition bar that was lower in calories. Sports enthusiasts said they wanted a high-protein bar that actually tasted good, and we came up with Clif Builders, which contains twenty grams of protein.

The point: We try to tap into unmet needs by personally spending time with consumers to discover where they feel underserved by the offerings in the market. We try to create products they desire and can't find anywhere else. These consumers recommend the product to others. We might attract more people initially if we spent lots of money in product launches; but many of these consumers won't stick around and we would have to keep spending money beyond our means to sustain the business. Instead we build loyalty by providing products a circle of consumers desire; over time we tap new circles and expand our consumer base. As a private company we can wait patiently for growth; this allows us breathing room so we can follow natural demand. Of course we will pull the plug if something doesn't work. However, if we see evidence of a strong natural demand for a truly innovative and profitable product we will give it time to catch on and grow.

We listen attentively to consumers to tap natural demand. We strive to follow natural demand rather than create artificial demand through massive advertising campaigns.

Innovation and Reinvention

Innovation remains central to who we are—we continually experiment to find the next "ah hah" and to surprise consumers with wonderful but unexpected nutritious treats. There are lots of examples: The Clif Bar itself changed the paradigm in the energy bar category from "bitter pill" to healthy, tasty, portable food. We began by creating flavors unique to the energy bar category, such as Carrot Cake, Chocolate Espresso, and Black Cherry Almond and continue to introduce new flavors on a regular basis for all our products, such as Luna's Dulce de Leche (a nondairy caramel) and Lemon Zest. Luna opened a new category—the first nutrition bar created for women. We created another new category with Mojo Bar, designed to be a healthy alternative to salty snacks heavy in bad fats, especially trans fats. In 2004, we introduced Clif Builders, a delicious multilayered, multi-textured bar that contains twice the protein, on average, of Clif Bar.

I told the company I wanted Clif to be like the Beatles. They quit singing "I Want to Hold Your Hand" early in their career

RAISING THE BAR

THE STORY OF CLIF BAR, INC.

because they were constantly evolving. We also continually reinvent ourselves to remain relevant to our consumers; staying true to the core of what our brands stand for, but reemerging in new ways. Clif Bar itself has gone through many reinventions. We update and improve our nutritional profile and ingredients: In 1999 we added more protein, fiber, and twenty-three vitamins and minerals to Clif Bar; in 2003 we converted all Clif Bars to organic. Luna, which stands for women's wellness, was reinvented when we added the Luna Glow, a low-carbohydrate bar, in response to women's demands.

It takes considerable resources and energy to create innovative, high-quality, nutritious products. Putting all that effort into a fad, which may only last a year or two, doesn't fit our goal of sustaining our brands over time—and we want to be leery of fads that don't enhance the health of our consumers. We try to identify trends, not fads, and create categories of product that fit the new context. A trend is a new way of viewing the world; something consumers will stick with for a while. For example, we waited to come out with low-carbohydrate bars, but once we realized that low-carbohydrate was a significant food trend rather than a fad, we moved quickly.

Nutrition and Quality Control

Clif products follow our food philosophy: "Sustaining People in Motion" with real food made from natural, nutritious ingredients. We buy our ingredients as close to the source as possible and choose components that haven't been heavily processed. That often means we buy smarter, negotiate harder, and are not afraid to spend more money to maintain the integrity of

OUR PHILOSOPHY OF FOOD—
SUSTAINING PEOPLE IN MOTION

At Clif Bar Inc., we delight in creating and savoring wholesome, delicious food. As bakers by trade and gourmet cooks on the side, we're energized by the joy people experience when they savor great food made with care. As athletes, we're committed to creating foods that sustain, nourish, and support people through any endeavor. As concerned individuals, we want our business to contribute to a healthier, more sustainable planet. These ideals inspire and motivate our work at Clif Bar, Inc.

Food that comes in a package can be wholesome. You shouldn't have to enlist a scientist to understand the ingredients on the product's label. From the beginning, our commitment has been to creating all-natural foods with no artificial flavors, colors, or preservatives. To that end, we use whole oats, fruits, nuts, and seeds. Our reason for doing so is simple: whole foods provide the most complete, balanced nutrition.

Natural foods also retain more antioxidants, phytonutrients, and essential vitamins and minerals than highly processed or refined foods. And research shows that natural, whole foods like Clif products are just as effective in delivering immediate and sustained energy for athletic performance as highly processed bars.

We strive to use organic ingredients in all of our products. Food grown organically—without the use of toxic pesticides or synthetic chemicals—is better for people and the environment. Supporting organic agriculture just makes sense. This gentler version of farming helps protect our water, air, soils, and wildlife from toxic substances, aids in preserving family farms, and moves us toward a more sustainable food system.

As a company and as individuals, we have a large impact on the planet. That's why we've embarked on this long-term road to sustainability to reduce our impact on the environment. We are examining every process and material—from the office products we use to the ingredients we source and the way we make our food. We want to be part of society's effort to restore and sustain our environment, and to support others who do so as well.

While achieving complete sustainability is only a dream at present, we commit to continue the journey.

our products. We could buy rice more cheaply from halfway around the world, but instead we buy where the best processing occurs, and we conduct research that tells us where that is and which growers take care of their land and people. We could use artificial flavors but refuse to make use of these chemicals, even if it would save us money. Back when our products contained coffee, we purchased beans from a single plantation cooperative in Costa Rica. We could certainly buy cheaper ingredients, but that would cost us the integrity and sustainability of our brand.

We have high standards of quality control to ensure the integrity of our brands. Many companies like ours, without their own plants, go to a manufacturer and say, "Make me a chocolate bar," and then the manufacturer doesn't see anyone from the contracting company until the bar is made. Too often, the contracting company doesn't use its own people to monitor the manufacture of the product. At Clif we have three full-time people in quality control who visit our bakeries constantly. This is in addition to the excellent lab analysis that the bakeries we contract conduct to ensure quality. We also use Clif employees to assist the quality assurance group in assessing every product. We *obsess* about taste; Clif people from all departments taste our products, thus allowing us to keep a close eye on product quality as well as developing expertise among a large group

" 'Are you nuts?' I remember thinking that when I heard Gary's philosophy on minimal advertising, no coupons in the Sunday newspaper, no slotting fees (the money you pay to get product on shelf). From my big company and business school experience, it had been ingrained in me that those are the foundational drivers of volume. Without those tools, increasing in expense year over year, the business would die.

But, luckily, I've always been a sponge for learning. And learn I did after that first experience of culture shock. I watched, I asked, I listened, I read, I explored, I experimented, and I began to realize that the world was not so black and white. I realized that when the rules of engagement change—so that it's not just about big immediate growth—and when there is a tolerance for risk, that the world of possibilities as to how to build a brand is endless. Also, I found that the compartment in my head where I had stored my creativity exploded open so that I was able to explore further and new ways of sustaining our brands became possible.

Now that we are bigger, I look for great people to be part of the fabric of our brand organization that are smart, driven, and have a good founda-tion of experience for how to build business. More important, I dig deep to understand if they have it at their core to explore and discover new ways. And, if they have the stomach for 'gray,' because no matter how experienced someone is, if they don't have 'it' in their gut, the person won't be right to sustain our brands. "

—SHERYL O'LOUGHLIN, CHIEF OF BRAND

of employees. This Clif panel of taste experts is called Fave Flave and panelists become experts in particular flavors. All our products must meet Clif's standards before they are shipped.

Connecting with Our Consumers

We try to connect at an intimate level with our consumers. We've always created traditional advertising, but our competitors outspend us as much as ten to one. We spend most of our energy, time, and money at the grassroots level—75 percent of the marketing department's budget goes to grassroots endeavors. Most companies either have tiny grassroots initiatives or they contract someone to do it for them; they think it's too expensive to do it in-house. That never felt right to us. We invest in this because we believe it's critical to make direct connections with our consumers. We want to learn what they are looking for, find out where we have screwed up, talk about our product, and tell our own story; no contracting company can do that. Clif marketing and field representatives around the country may host fifty to a hundred events on any given weekend. The thousand-plus athletes a year that we sponsor become Clif ambassadors. The point is that we constantly talk to consumers face-to-face, literally thousands of them every weekend, always finding and creating new ways of connecting to people.

We still rely on word of mouth to tell our story. It might not make conventional marketing sense to sponsor LunaFest, a women's film festival. After all, LunaFest only reaches a few thousand people and is pretty expensive to run. Our hope is that people who attend the film festival will be inspired to tell others about the films, The Breast Cancer Fund (which LunaFest supports), and yes, our bars as well! The Mountain Town Ambassadors Program supported athletes in little mountain towns, backing events that other companies ignore. It also allowed us to hang out in mountain towns and meet people, and if someone was cold on a lift we would give them a hat or a hot chocolate from Clif Bar. Again, sponsoring small regional events may not be cost-effective, but we want to give back to the outdoor enthusiasts who support Clif.

Would everything I've discussed about brand be different if we were a red-road company? I think so. If we traveled the red road we'd look at what is hot on the market and say, "Ingredient X is hot. Let's create something with Ingredient X and push it." We'd go to low-cost manufacturers and tell them, "Make us an X bar." They would tell us what flavors they could make and produce the bar in the cheapest way possible. We'd go to package people and say, "Make us a package." We'd do a strong launch, spending $10–20 million on advertising, emphasizing radio, print, maybe even some television. On the red road we'd use cheap ingredients, traditional marketing, big advertising dollars, and heavy promotions at retail outlets—the tried-and-true formula.

Clif started with a natural, authentic product. We want to keep our mojo for the long haul and believe we can do that by attending carefully to natural demand, using ingredients that help us tread lightly on the earth, and staying intimately connected to our consumers.

> **SECOND ASPIRATION**
SUSTAINING OUR BUSINESS—
LIVING WITHIN OUR MEANS

A company, like an individual, needs to live within its means. We don't believe in borrowing lots of money to grow the business. We believe in maintaining private ownership rather than building a company in order to sell it (the norm in corporate America). We feel an obligation to our employees and our consumers to make sure Clif Bar Inc. is viable and lasting. So we don't push Clif Bar to grow unnaturally, but rather to sustain itself over time.

Extraction, Reinvestment, Profit

As Clif shareholders, we can only expect a modest financial return on our investment—that is, if we want to sustain our business. We can't extract so much from Clif Bar that it affects the company's health. If we did that, there would be no money left to cushion the business. Read the business section of the newspaper on any given day, and you'll find stories of CEOs with exorbitant benefit and compensation packages. We don't want to be high-flying CEOs taking outrageous amounts of money out of the business. We want our actions to support the long-term health of the company.

Clif Bar doesn't exist for profit, but we can't live without it. Jim Collins writes in *Good to Great* that profit is the blood and water of a company. You don't say "I live for blood," but blood keeps you alive. I believe profit is necessary as a means to other ends and is important in the early life cycle of any business.

OUR BUSINESS ASPIRATIONS

SUSTAINING OUR BUSINESS
LIVING WITHIN OUR MEANS

May our business survive and thrive for future generations as a healthy company that is viable, vibrant, and lasting. To accomplish this long-term vision we will remain privately held to control our destiny. While remaining privately held we choose a rate of growth that is governed by our ability to live within our means.

This approach creates a long-term sustainable business model. It's a model of patience versus greed. It's not about short-term gain. It's about long-term health. And remaining healthy as a business gives us the power to support and steward our brands, our people, our community, and the planet.

ALWAYS – ATTENTIVE, ADAPTIVE, ACTIVE

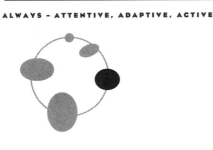

*All facts and information subject to improve.

Nutrition Facts*
Yearly Compilation of Activities

Activity   1yr. Difference

Activity	1yr. Difference
Net Sales	Up 24%
Gross Margin	Up 4%
EBITDA	Up 66%
Inventory Levels	3 Days Lower
Liabilities payables	10 Days Lower
Collections DSO	5 Days Lower

INGREDIENTS
Refinance debt, free cashflow (w/ added working capital management), tax planning, lower cost of goods, regular budget reviews (with re-alignment of spend to sales), low inventory levels, investing in training and education.

Fortunately, Clif Bar Inc. was profitable in its first year and continues to be so.

Our profit margin is what's left after we take out the cost of the product and the selling, general, and administrative costs (SG&A)—basically, all overhead costs. We also use EBITDA, earnings before interest, taxes, depreciation, and amortization, to gauge the health of our company. We build in margins for our products that allow us to pay our expenses and provide some cushion for the company in case things don't go as expected. Our goal is a margin large enough to cushion us during seasonal down cycles and allow us to invest a percentage of our profit back into the company each year.

A sustainable company must ensure enough of a margin to reinvest in the business. Most profits must be reinvested in the company.

Rate of Growth

A red-road company sets growth targets based on what shareholders or investors determine annual returns *should* be. The company then has to create sufficient consumer demand to hustle up the revenues to meet growth projections. This necessitates a capital-intensive marketing plan: lots of money is spent *engineering* demand rather than supporting *actual* demand. I believe the rate of growth should be determined by natural demand.

Clif supports natural demand rather than creating artificial demand. Our management team sets sales targets based on demonstrable product demand, which is projected using the actual pipeline of product orders, future order estimates, and estimated consumer movement. When launching new products, we try to project modestly and build in a cushion. We launched the Mojo Bar, forecasting $4 million in sales for the first year and $9 million for the second. It turned out that we only hit $2.3 million during Mojo's first year. We adjusted our projections quickly and realized that at best we'd hit $1.2 million the second year. Obviously, we didn't make money on Mojo, but thanks to our careful spending, we didn't sink the ship either. Since we hadn't overinvested we were able to pull back the following year, cut our costs, and take time to decide if we wanted to re-launch Mojo or bag it. After analyzing our mistakes, we re-launched Mojo with a new package and new flavors in a conservative regional rollout to test the natural demand that we still believed existed. We let consumers determine whether the product was viable.

Given our philosophy of natural demand, how do we think about growth? We have three options: We could aim to level out at our present size and rate of sales. We could aim to grow fast and hard. Or we could look for a balance between the first two options. In the end, I prefer a balanced approach for a variety of reasons. People at Clif are competitive, as you have learned in this book. We like to ride in the break. We get excited about creating and innovating. Our growth provides career opportunities for our employees, and a no-growth policy would be like holding back a racehorse. We perform best when we compete, but we have to balance our competitive nature with growth that is sustainable. If we grow too fast we risk the five aspirations that make up the Clif ecosystem. We protect ourselves by not pursuing outrageous rates of growth.

" I steward the business by helping achieve Clif Bar's financial and operational plan. Since everything works in concert (you don't make your profit without getting the sales, which means ordering the right inventory, which means collecting cash, and so on), I have to be part of a team. We don't believe in one-person shows at Clif Bar. I spend a lot of time explaining finance to non-financial people to help the team make well-rounded decisions. Likewise, I myself spend a great deal of time trying to understand everything from R&D to Marketing. Good teamwork takes the mystery out of other people's work.

Being flexible with my thinking helps a lot too. I try to be ready to change direction and have always had a backup plan. It's a bit like steering a sailboat to the dock. You have to contend with the unexpected gust of wind, the floating log in the water, to get your boat safely to the dock. "

—STAN TANKA, CHIEF OF FINANCE

Business as Stewardship

I see the role of the chief financial officer (CFO) as similar to
that of a farmer who conscientiously stewards the land—and
all that grows or lives on it—to keep it healthy. Stewarding a
business means attending to commonsense principles, paying
constant attention to profit and loss and cash flow, managing
inventory and receivables, and protecting the gross margins.
Stan Tanka, our CFO, had his ear to the ground during our off
year, attending closely to financial and banking markets. This
attentiveness enabled us to refinance our debt a third time with
Bank of America as lead bank and Union Bank of California at
a rate of about 4 percent, saving us $8 million in interest. SPP
again brokered the deal.

I think businesspeople and shareholders forgot the benefits of
good stewardship during the 1990s. They expected their stocks
to soar within a short period of time; they anticipated wealth
beyond their wildest dreams, quickly. If the company disappeared, so be it—as long as their riches didn't. It's clear now
that a market based on excessive expectations can't sustain
itself. Ordinary investors in a company guided by a long-term
sustainable business plan might not become multimillionaires,
but they could probably count on retiring with an adequate
income. My parents never invested in stocks; they invested in a
modest pension plan from the state. Their pension allows them
to pay their bills, with enough left over to do the things that
make them happy. They're having the time of their lives! Most
people aren't greedy; they want to be able to live decently and
retire with security.

RAISING THE BAR · THE STORY OF CLIF BAR, INC.

Today, in the wake of the poor stewardship of the 1990s, many elderly people are forced out of retirement or survive on radically diminished incomes. They put their money into companies over which they didn't have any control, and some of those companies went bust because a few people favored short-term profit over sustainable growth. Successful companies follow long-term sustainable business models. They create products with demand, they remain profitable, they build in cushions, and they have plans for succession. Great companies commit to good stewardship.

Corporate America is too often about quick profit. That bottom line is incompatible with long-term sustainable growth.

➤ **THIRD ASPIRATION**
SUSTAINING OUR PEOPLE—
LIVE LIFE TO ITS FULLEST
We are a company that cares about each other like no other company I've seen. We are gay, straight, athletes, couch potatoes, musicians, tone deaf, black, white, Latino, we are everything. I've come home.
—CLIF EMPLOYEE

Take care of your people. Create and sustain a business where they can live, not just make a living. Before Clif Bar was up for sale, people came to the company saying, "I want this to be my last stop." When I came close to selling, I couldn't look them in the eyes. I know now that I have a responsibility to the people of Clif Bar. Their well-being is critical. Businesses often talk about taking care of their people. In reality, they see this as a means to an end: The better you treat people, the harder they

OUR BUSINESS ASPIRATIONS

SUSTAINING OUR PEOPLE
LIVE LIFE TO ITS FULLEST

May our business be around for future generations to provide a place for people to contribute, learn and grow while they live the life they want to live. We will always remember that our company is alive with passionate, intelligent, creative, and responsible human beings and that it is our job to inspire them to do their best.

People thrive in our environment when we consider and nourish the whole person – body, mind, heart, and soul. Our employees are not a means to an end. Our people are our company.

ALWAYS – ATTENTIVE, ADAPTIVE, ACTIVE

*All facts and information subject to improve.

Nutrition Facts*
Annual Compilation of Activities

Activity 1yr. Difference

Activity	1yr. Difference
Massages	480
Gym Classes	71,000
Epiphany Ride (total miles)	6,782
Cars Washed	>500
Thursday Morning Meetings	52
Giants Home Games	81

INGREDIENTS
Annual Incentive Plan, Epiphany Ride, Martini & Weenie Party, company picnic, camping trip, ski trip, SF Giants season tickets, 40 Iron Chef cook-offs, gym, wellness program, concierge services, fabulous holiday party, sabbatical leave, 9/80 workweek, bagel, donuts, music concerts.

will work. In my opinion, that's just another version of bottom-line thinking. People spend 2,080 hours a year at the work-place. We believe that if we provide meaningful work as well as something *beyond* work, people will do their jobs well *and* lead healthier, more balanced lives.

Find and Retain the Right People

The first step in sustaining our people is to hire the right folks in the first place. Of course, anyone applying for a position at Clif needs to show that they have the skills for the job, but we also look for other skills that allow someone to feel good about working with us and to add their own special something to the culture. Human Resources relies on intuition, as well as the instincts of the group doing the hiring, to bring in new employ-ees who have the right skills. If new employees want the red road, they won't last long. We want people who are drawn to Clif Bar because of our reputation, our products, and our val-ues. We want people who are willing to travel the white road.

Compensation

In 2002, one company homework assignment was to read and discuss *Twenty-Two Immutable Laws of Branding* by Al and Laura Ries. In a related assignment we explored why people chose to be at Clif Bar by creating a business version of Maslow's hierarchy. According to Maslow, basic needs such as food and water must be provided before people can appreciate great music or join social causes. I met to discuss the book and the hierarchy with groups of five or six people over a succession of lunches. After we discussed the book, I asked people to tell me

" I believe in art, intuition, and instinct, which probably distinguishes me from a lot of HR people. I am suspicious of metrics, performance measures, and studies that attempt to reduce employees, and the many human interactions that occur in the workplace and in the employment life cycle—from recruiting to hiring to firing—to a set of formulae, measures, and models from corporate gurus. I believe that at the end of the day everyone wants to do a good job and be successful, and that it is my job to select people who are likely to be successful in our environment. Once they're here, it's my job to provide a fair compensation and benefits package, meaningful work, opportunities for personal growth, and a few surprises that say to employees, 'Clif Bar values you and your contribution to the success of the business.' "

–DAVID JERICOFF, VICE PRESIDENT OF HUMAN RESOURCES

RAISING THE BAR

THE STORY OF CLIF BAR, INC.

their basic reasons for working at Clif Bar. Not surprisingly, I discovered that, although people enjoy having a gym, receiving massages, even getting their eyebrows plucked, these perks were not the main reason they came to Clif Bar. Compensation, like Maslow's food and water, was a basic reason.

It is critically important that we pay fair market rates, and to do so takes ongoing diligence. Thao Pham, director of Human Resources, analyzes market rates in the San Francisco Bay Area every six months to ensure that our salaries remain fair. We try to offer the best possible compensation package, including benefits, that we can for a company our size. In lieu of employee stock options, Clif Bar gives an annual bonus based on the company's performance as well as employee performance. We provide medical, dental, and vision coverage, life and disability insurance, and we match employee contributions in our Clif 401(k) Savings Plan. Another "basic need" is housing, a thorny issue here in the San Francisco Bay Area. So, for first-time homebuyers, we offer cash loans to match what they already have for a down payment, at low interest rates.

Learning and Growing

We find ways for people to continue learning and growing. One way we do this is to have a Career Development Center, which brings in outside experts to teach an array of classes, in-house. Employees also enjoy learning from each other. In my life this kind of learning counted far more than any formal class. I learned a lot at California Polytechnic University, but my real education took place on the job. At Clif Bar we encourage people to take risks, try new things, and learn from great people with years of experience. There are lots of examples: Tom Richardson was too busy being a world-class rock climber to go to college. He started packing for trade shows, took every opportunity for on-the-job learning, and is now in Research and Development. Brandon Floyd also started in the warehouse, moved into sales, and now he's a sales forecasting coordinator. People can grow in their careers at Clif Bar.

Wellness—Work Hard, Play Hard, Recover

My worst cycling years were the ones in which I *over* trained: I'd perform well in spring races, but come summer I'd be blown out. In reaction I'd train harder and ride more miles, going deeper into deficit until I couldn't recover. By the time I quit the season I'd be depressed, performing poorly, and, boy, would I hate training! Athletes and their trainers have figured out that it's not the quantity but the quality of your workout. If you work too hard and too long, it takes you twice as long to recover. Top athletes strive for a balance between training and performing, rest and recovery. I think people in business follow a similar pattern. I've witnessed people grind away at their desks for four hours straight without taking a break, even a bathroom break. At Clif Bar we want people to work hard, but employees also need to figure out ways to rest and recover. It may be taking a walk around the block, heading down to Bette's Oceanview Diner for a cup of coffee, going to the gym, getting a massage, taking a yoga or spinning class, or going to our quiet room to kick back in a chair and listen to music. We want to help employees find their optimal work and recovery cycle.

RAISING
THE
BAR

THE STORY OF CLIF BAR, INC.

CLIF GYM AND DANCE STUDIO. —PAUL MCKENZIE

We need rest and recovery as a company too. For a number of years I worked in Italy at the bike seat company, Selle Italia. Selle Italia, like many European businesses, closes for the holidays. I learned that if individuals need vacations to recover, companies do too. So we shut the office at Clif Bar from December 25 through New Year's. Some people are tempted to call the office while on vacation, but you can resist the temptation when there's no one there to answer your call! The holiday break is the company's, not the individual's, so it doesn't count against personal vacation time. It is Clif's time of renewal.

Clif also offers a sabbatical program. Every seven years an individual is eligible for a three-month paid sabbatical, with the possibility of extending the sabbatical an additional three months without pay. In this way employees have the opportunity to explore other parts of their lives. Chelseah took up tap dancing and traveled in Panama and Costa Rica (her first trip out of the United States). Cassandra returned to school and got a jump-start on a college degree. Daniel reconnected with his first love, music, and then realized that he needed to follow his own white road: He took up music, full time. We wished him well on his journey, although we were sad to lose him.

The Clif Wellness Program addresses employees' physical, emotional, even spiritual needs. Janet Minix, our "Wellness Diva," organizes a wide range of services. You'll find play stations as well as workstations inside our expansive warehouse-like building. We have a state-of-the-art gym, a dance studio, and a two-story climbing wall. Clif Bar offers more than twenty fitness classes per week, during working hours. Classes in 2003 included spinning, kickboxing, fat burn, circuit training, walking, running, weight lifting, chi gung, martial arts, Pilates, stretching, step aerobic, dance aerobic, strength training, and yoga. Personal trainers are available for one-on-one sessions throughout the week, as well as for weekend training rides. Clif Bar employees get paid for staying in shape—at the rate of two-and-a-half hours of workout time per week. Currently, Janet estimates that 97 percent of employees participate in the fitness program.

Many of our employees would like to go straight home to their families after work, rather than doing time-consuming errands. Clif started a Concierge Services program to shorten employees' days and alleviate stress. The program, offered at low cost to employees, provides laundry and dry cleaning pick-up and delivery twice a week. Clif also has an on-site washing machine and dryer for employees' personal use. A hair stylist comes to Clif to cut hair. Griffin Motorwerke will pick up, service, and deliver cars back to the Clif Bar parking lot. An auto detailer comes in on Thursdays to wash, wax, or detail employees' cars. We've contracted with a caterer who will cook dinners for employees and deliver the meals to the workplace. Top masseuses offer massages twice a week. It's our hope that these services shorten our employees' workdays and relieve stress.

We take play seriously at Clif Bar! We have a playroom with a pool table, shuffleboard, and a place to hit golf balls. We organize weekly basketball games and tournaments at our company basketball court. Ski trips, camping and rock climbing trips, the annual Martini & Weenie party, the holiday bash, family

" I arrived at Clif Bar in April 1999, after I retired from twenty-plus years at a Fortune 500 company. At the end of my second year of retirement, I realized I was not ready to hang up my administrative shoes yet. I found my way to Clif Bar. Oh what a place! The day I interviewed there were two dogs roaming around the office. I remember hoping they wouldn't bark or bite me! People were walking around in flip-flops and cut-off jeans, or they had on workout clothes with towels around their necks. It looked like utter chaos, but the place was alive, and you could see that business was happening. I wanted to be part of what was happening.

There was no wellness program when I joined Clif Bar. We had a small, well-equipped gym with two trainers and a head coach. I spent quite a bit of time with the trainers and asked them if they would offer different classes and maybe bring in instructors to teach kickboxing or yoga. The physical fitness component of the program grew. The next phase of the program was the health side of the wellness program. Now roughly 89 percent of all Berkeley-based employees participate in one or more of the health screens we offer. And, finally the Concierge component was a nat-ural addition. We were working them out and screening their health. The final ingredient the company could offer was to reduce their daily stress.

What will be next? On-site dentistry? Mobile dog groomers? I don't know. I survey the employees, I check wellness Web sites, and I look under rocks for ways to support Clif Bar folks. I just know that I am so fortunate to have the opportunity to be the Wellness Manager for Clif Bar. This is an experience I will never forget. "

—JANET MINIX, WELLNESS DIVA

RAISING
THE BAR

THE STORY OF CLIF BAR, INC.

picnics, the Annual Epiphany Ride, and weekly Bagels and Donuts are just a few ways that employees recreate together. Participation in company events is high. One of the great joys of owning this business is seeing how people enjoy being together.

I believe we should lead balanced lives. Sometimes people need to burn the midnight oil at Clif, but generally the office is empty by five or six. In addition, we have the 9/80 Program: For every two weeks, employees work nine rather than ten days. This means that everyone has a three-day weekend, every other weekend, in which to climb, ski, bicycle, travel, rest, or spend time with family and friends.

Meaning and Purpose in Work

I have never worked for a company with a conscience before.

—CLIF EMPLOYEE

During the book and Maslow discussions, people told me they felt good about their work because they believed in what Clif was doing. Employees respect that we make values-based decisions. Many ranked our community service program and the sustainability initiative right at the top of their list of reasons for staying at Clif Bar. Some even ranked the company's values on a par with salary. They found meaning in their work, which made them want to be at Clif Bar.

I think that participating in grassroots marketing makes people's work more meaningful. Anyone in the company can go to the events that Clif sponsors: LunaFest, an outdoor cycling race, a marathon—you name it. An employee who wants to run a marathon might go a day early to work in the Clif booth and get a chance to talk with our consumers face-to-face. People who do this can see the joy in consumers' eyes and directly experience the results of their hard work. We encourage everyone, in all parts of the company, to make direct contact with our public because it deepens their understanding of and commitment to our work.

Morale

Keeping an eye on morale is a top priority at Clif Bar. Unhappy employees don't bring their full energy and creativity to their work and they affect office relationships negatively. Fair compensation, meaningful work, values, personal growth and learning, working hard and playing hard, good relationships, all affect morale positively.

Growing—and growing up—is a fact of life if your business is successful. In 1994, Clif Bar Inc. ended the year with six employees. At the end of 2003, 140 people worked at Clif. People understandably felt anxious as we grew and changed. Some wondered if our values would change, others felt uncomfortable with new people coming in from large corporations. People wondered if Clif would stay on course as they watched me hand over more of the daily operations to key management. We were no longer the small team fighting to win a tournament.

With growth comes change to the corporate culture. If growth and change are not managed with extreme care, it affects your most important business asset, your people. We attend to morale because we know that it can break down quickly.

Sustaining our people is central to our business model. A good and healthy place to work is a worthy return on investment. A cool, fun place to work is an end in itself. We want employees to lead full and balanced lives.

➤ FOURTH ASPIRATION
SUSTAINING OUR COMMUNITY—GIVING BACK

Clif Bar is a gift. I always hoped that it would be successful, but never in my wildest dreams did I think it would become so big. Kit and I know that it never could have happened without the give-and-take between Clif and a wider circle—family, friends, vendors, retailers, consumers, and well-wishers. We believe in giving back to the community that nurtured us and that continues to help us grow. During one of our many conversations about return on investment, Kit said, "Clif Bar has the power to do good things." She saw that Clif Bar has more power to influence, change, and give back to the community than we would, had we sold the company.

SUSTAINING OUR COMMUNITY
GIVING BACK

May our community grow as future generations are inspired by our desire to be a "Business with Heart," and may we remember the heroism of those we support. May the compassion, creativity, and courage that define the foundation of our involvement continue to shape our vision of the future and to reflect the legacy of our company.

As a living part of our community, a portion of the money we earn and the hours we work will always serve to support and improve environmental, social, and cultural needs, from our local to our global community. Serving our community and supporting important causes is not a by-product, but an aspiration of our business.

ALWAYS - ATTENTIVE, ADAPTIVE, ACTIVE

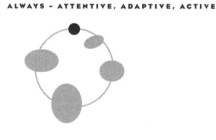

*All facts and information subject to improve.

Nutrition Facts*
Annual Compilation of Activities

Activity 1yr. Difference

Meals Delivered	792
Animals Saved	2
Boxes of Food Packed	504
BORP Ride Miles	144
Trails Preserved	>5
Insulin Shots Administered	4,275
Bikes Donated	32
2 x 4's Nailed	2,000

INGREDIENTS
Santa Clara Co. Diabetes Society, The Breast Cancer Peak Hike, Habitat for Humanity, Sports for Kids, Ma & Pa Green, Bay Area Outreach Recreation Program, Friends of Five Creeks, Meals on Wheels, Adopt-A-Trail, AIDS Walk, PAWS, Cinderella Ride, Circle of Life, Disabled Sports USA, Alameda Co. Food Bank, Peralta Elementary School, East Bay Fire Fighters, East Bay Pride, Rose Day, Georgetown High School, Brower Youth, Read Aloud Day, Berkeley Booster, Markie Foundation, Leukemia & Lymphoma Society.

Giving to our community is one of Clif's five core aspirations; it's not something we do because we have a little extra profit each year. A portion of the money we make and the hours we work will always go to support community causes. We are part of local and global communities and aspire to be responsible citizens.

Do No Harm

All too often American tourists are rude and insensitive to local cultures. My buddy Jay and I tried to be good global citizens on our bike trips. We truly appreciated people and their cultures, and we wanted to act respectfully. Likewise, Clif Bar tries to be sensitive to our neighbors in Berkeley, California—to be a good citizen. David Batstone, in *Saving the Corporate Soul,* urges companies to "think of [themselves] as part of a community as well as a market." A business should be a part of, rather than dominate, its locale. People live right across the street from our office; it's important that we listen to our neighbors. We don't spew toxins into our neighborhood. Before we initiate any plan that could affect the surrounding area, we inform the community. We believe that we should be transparent to the nearby area.

2080 Program—Giving Our Time

From the start, philanthropic efforts were important to Lisa (my former business partner) and to me. Over the years we've supported numerous causes—including AIDS work, environmental groups, and health-related organizations—by giving free samples of our products, the sweat equity of our employees, and cash contributions. We've paid Clif people to deliver meals to AIDS patients, pound nails for Habitat for Humanity, clean

CLIF PEOPLE BUILDING WITH HABITAT FOR
HUMANITY, OAKLAND, CALIFORNIA.
—GARY ERICKSON

" I believe that giving back to our community is a privilege, and I will always value the experiences of helping others. Through our 2080 Program, we have been touched by the warm smiles, the hearty laughs, and the tears of joy and sadness of those we have helped—whether it is a small child facing diabetes or a senior citizen enjoying her warm meal. They have all inspired us to be more courageous and have taught us to be humble. I think it is important that we should all want to give back to the community.

I can't imagine Clif Bar without community service. I really tried picturing Clif Bar without community service and I couldn't. It's Clif Bar—a group of caring people. "

—THAO PHAM, DIRECTOR OF HUMAN RESOURCES,
IN CHARGE OF THE 2080 PROGRAM

beaches with Surfrider Foundation, serve meals in soup kitchens, and teach people to read. In 1999, two-thirds of the company participated in various AIDS Rides as riders or support staff. Clif Bar paid for the participation and didn't count the time away from the office against employee vacation time.

In the early years, our decisions about how and where to participate were more informal and spontaneous, but in 2001 a creative and dedicated group of employees got together and decided it was time for Clif to formalize its volunteer program—and Project 2080 was born. We initially committed 2080 employee hours annually (the equivalent of one full-time employee) to causes selected by our employees. In 2004, we converted the formula to 20.8 paid hours per person per year and expanded our service program to include international options, offering employees the opportunity to volunteer in emerging countries. The international option gives our employees a firsthand look at the complicated challenges facing women, men, and children in impoverished communities throughout the world at the same time that they make tangible contributions to communities in need.

Do we need community service to sustain our brand and business? Probably not. We could survive, in the traditional sense, without it, but doing so would take some of Clif's soul away. Community service is important to who we are as a company. I believe it also contributes to sustaining our people. It's a blast to hammer nails, paint, and hang out with people from all over the company while building a house for Habitat for Humanity. Employees from different departments get to spend time together while they support dozens of different organizations.

Camaraderie develops among volunteers, and they end up feeling good about themselves and their company. Clif people are dedicated and committed. I consider myself fortunate to know them. Social consciousness percolates throughout our company.

Partnerships and Sponsorships

When considering sponsorships we ask three questions: Do we truly believe in the cause? Can we really help the organization we're sponsoring? Will the work we do in common provide direct marketing opportunities and help strengthen our brands as well as the brands of the groups we sponsor? The way Luna works with The Breast Cancer Fund (TBCF) is a perfect example of how Clif sponsorship works. First, breast cancer hits very close to home—my mother is a survivor and the disease has touched many of our employees personally. Second, the way TBCF approaches the issue matches our own passionate beliefs—The Fund identifies and advocates for the elimination of environmental and other preventable causes of breast cancer. Clif's sponsorship helps TBCF in a variety of concrete ways— Luna places The Breast Cancer Fund logo on the wrappers of all bars sold nationwide, provides TBCF materials at numerous Luna events throughout the country, and donates employee time and Luna bars to various TBCF fundraisers. In addition, a portion of the proceeds of Luna sales goes directly to The Breast Cancer Fund, making us the fund's largest single donor. We assist the fund at special fundraising events, including the inspiring Climb Against the Odds, where breast cancer survivors and their supporters climb Mount Shasta in northern California. Clif's sponsorship increases the visibility of The

Breast Cancer Fund and contributes directly and concretely to its work. Finally, by helping a cause we believe in and affiliating with an incredible group, we strengthen our brand.

We also partner with the Leukemia & Lymphoma Society, another cause that hits close to home: Greg Vette, a dear friend of both Lois and me, died from non-Hodgkin's Lymphoma in the fall of 2002. Another close friend, Spider Cantley, dedicates his life to this cause. We participate in the annual radio station KGO Cure-a-Thon (founded by Spider) in San Francisco, as well as in Team in Training, a national athletic program that supports the society. The athletes who train to participate in fundraising events for the Leukemia & Lymphoma Society receive product and donations from us.

We have sponsored more than a thousand sports and charity events over the years. Sponsorships give exposure to the company and the brand. More important, they are a concrete way to give back to the community.

Product and Cash

We give away *lots* of bars every year. We're proud that we have a healthy product to donate to worthy causes. We gave over one million bars to support different organizations and causes during 2003. When El Salvador suffered a devastating earthquake we immediately sent bars. We give bars to local and national food banks on an ongoing basis. My brother-in-law, Andrew Hayes, is a social worker. He comes by the office regularly to pick up bars for homeless shelters in San Francisco. We assist

RAISING THE BAR

THE STORY OF CLIF BAR, INC.

numerous groups that care for and feed the elderly and under-privileged children in the Bay Area and across the country. We donate a large volume of product to employee-supported chari-ties and events. We also donate specially designed bicycles, driven by hand cranks, for use by paraplegic cyclists. We initi-ated a buddy system in which a rider from Clif Bar shadows a cyclist who is riding one of these special bikes.

Clif established the rripL^3 Fund, a grant program that supports groups in the areas of *community, culture,* and the *earth.* The rripL^3 Fund tends to fund smaller grassroots organizations. We believe that these small, scrappy groups often give the biggest "bang for the buck" and that funders frequently overlook them. The rripL^3 Fund sponsors Project Wild Hope, which Dave Willis operates on a shoestring budget. Wild Hope has struggled for years to protect a crucial ecological wild land in southern Ore-gon where the Siskiyou Mountains join the Cascade Range. Thanks to the efforts of Dave and the Soda Mountain Wilder-ness Council, President Clinton turned 52,951 public acres into the Cascade-Siskiyou National Monument. The rripL^3 Fund also gladly sponsors Patricia Reedy's Luna Kids Dance (named before our bar came out!). Patricia provides movement experi-ences and dance instruction for low-income mothers and their children. All employees also can pick a charity of their choice and the rripL^3 Fund matches their donations. The rripL^3 Fund proudly contributes to numerous nonprofit organizations.

Influencing Others

Companies like Timberland, Ben & Jerry's, Patagonia, and Working Assets influenced how I think about the role of a company in a community. Timberland offers employees forty hours of paid leave annually and three-to-six month "service" sabbaticals. Patagonia's Employee Internship Program offers up to two months of paid leave to work full time for the environmental group of the employee's choice; more than 350 employees have interned for groups worldwide since the program began. We want our 2080 Program, rripL³ Fund, and community partnerships to influence other companies. Our hope is that more businesses will see the many benefits to be gained from strong community service and outreach. Every company should be a good corporate citizen, transparent to its community, its neighbors, and its consumers. If Clif Bar, by its humble example, exercises even a modest influence on other businesses and the community, we gain a valuable return on our investment.

We exist due to the support of a community. The least we can do is give back.

> **FIFTH ASPIRATION**
> **SUSTAINING THE PLANET—**
> **REDUCING OUR ECOLOGICAL FOOTPRINT**

I'm not a trained environmentalist, but I'm willing to face facts, and the facts show that human beings are screwing up the earth and that business practices are to blame for a lot of environmental damage. I don't want Clif Bar to further damage the planet. I want to know how what we do affects life downstream. As I discussed in Chapter Three, we started a company-wide sustainability program in 2001 and hired Elysa Hammond as staff ecologist to guide us. The long-term goal of the Clif Bar Environmental Program is to reduce our ecological footprint

RAISING
THE BAR

THE STORY OF CLIF BAR, INC.

OUR BUSINESS ASPIRATIONS

SUSTAINING THE PLANET
REDUCING OUR ECOLOGICAL FOOTPRINT

May our company now and in future generations help to preserve and heal the planet. We recognize the need to be good stewards of all natural resources. We work to reduce our ecological footprint in everything we do as a business, from the field to the final product.

We want to do business in a way that promotes long-term solutions to environmental problems, maintains the integrity of natural ecosystems, and conserves and improves the quality of air, water, and soils.

ALWAYS – ATTENTIVE, ADAPTIVE, ACTIVE

*All facts and information subject to improve.

Nutrition Facts*
Annual Compilation of Activities
Category   1yr. Impact

Clif Bar USDA certified 70% Organic
Organic ingredients purchased 7,000,000 lbs.

Green Purchasing:

Recycled paperboard	1,440,000 lbs.
(10,000,000 caddies / year)	

Environmental benefits:

Water saved (gallons)	3,300,000
Trees saved	7,500
Greenhouse gasses avoided	660,000 lbs.

Recycled paper	87,000 lbs.

Environmental benefits:

Water saved (gallons)	150,000
Trees saved	570
Greenhouse gasses avoided	47,800 lbs.

Green Power program:

Wind energy purchased	3,228,974 kWh
(kilowatt hours (kWh) of green tags)	
Lbs. of CO_2 emissions offset	5,500,000

INGREDIENTS
Clif Newsletter (Moving Toward Sustainability), organic initiative, 100% recycled, shrinkwrap-free caddies, New Leaf Recycled Paper, *Native*Energy *Wind*builders, Clean Air-Cool Planet, EPA Green Power Program, organic cotton T-shirts, Clif Eco-Posse, SF Precautionary Principle Ordinance, Stop Waste Environmental audit, Co-op America, Bioneers, Green Festivals, American Forests.

along every step of the production process, from the field to the final product.

We don't claim great expertise. We are just one company with a desire to learn, partner with, and support other businesses and groups that share this vision. We hope we can inspire other companies to support sustainable agriculture, organic farming, and a healthier food system. We are a small company that wants to act responsibly so our grandchildren's children will thrive on this planet.

Sustainable Ingredients

I believe it's important to understand where our food comes from and how it is grown. Agricultural production has an impact on the environment, the lives of farmers and farm workers, and the quality of the food we eat. At Clif we're committed to supporting farming methods that safeguard the health of our soil and water resources, protect biodiversity, avoid the use of toxic chemicals, and reduce our contribution to global warming.

Our approach is to analyze our impact as far upstream as possible, and that means starting with farm production. The core of our environmental program is a commitment to organic agriculture. Organically grown ingredients are produced without synthetic pesticides or fertilizers and without the use of sewage sludge, irradiation, or genetically modified organisms. Organic farmers protect biodiversity through crop rotation, use of beneficial insects, soil conservation, water pollution prevention, and by maintaining a healthy soil microbial community. We support farms that comply with national organic standards. Of course,

" I love my job. I'm an ecosystem ecologist with an interest in sustainable food systems. Working at Clif Bar I have the opportunity to put ecological theories into practice. And it's working. Our program is alive and growing. We're creating a greener, more environmentally sound company along every step of the production process. Above all, people are learning that the most important step in working toward a healthier, more sustainable food system is to support organic agriculture. That point is foundational.

I've spent most of the past twenty years working in research and education in a variety of places including farmers' fields in Mexico, Peru, and Indonesia, and with children and college students in New York. The work has been varied but always linked by one common thread—connecting the dots between food, agriculture, and the environment. Three years ago I started as staff ecologist for Clif Bar, a job that evolved out of conversations I had with Gary about agriculture many years ago. Our goal is to truly build an ecological company, one that works in harmony with nature and that conserves our planet's resources for the long haul. It's a long-term commitment and a lofty vision but it makes going to work interesting and fun and encouraging, not just for me but for many employees. And that's important because it takes a passionate group of people, not a single person, to make things happen. "

—ELYSA HAMMOND, CLIF ECOLOGIST

we do not use genetically modified ingredients in any of our products.

It was an arduous but exhilarating process to convert Clif Bar to organic. We had to analyze each ingredient and search for available organic alternatives. When we converted to organic rice to make brown rice syrup, we purchased 5 percent of the entire U.S. organic rice crop. Clif Bar is a small business; this shows the impact one company can have on the environment when it changes just one ingredient! We estimate that in 2004 we will use seven million pounds of organic ingredients from thousands of acres of farmland. We're proud that Clif Bar is certified organic, and we continue to look deeply into our supply chain to find ingredients produced with organic or sustainable methods for all our products. Our plan is to increase the organic content of our brands to at least 70 percent on average.

Sustainable agriculture also can promote the just treatment of farm workers. Recently, Bob Scowcroft, executive director of the Organic Farming Research Foundation, told Elysa and me how farming organically not only affects farm owners' relationships with the soil but also with farm workers. To succeed, an organic farmer needs workers who know the land and crops intimately *over time;* organic farming needs informed, experienced workers who can spot a pest problem before it gets out of hand. Organic farmers must cultivate long-term relationships with farm workers. You can see this trend happening across the organic board, including on large commercial organic farms. Earth Bound Farms, one of the biggest providers of organic produce in the United States, trains many of its workers in organic farming methods. To me, organic farming is not just about getting rid of

RAISING THE BAR

THE STORY OF CLIF BAR, INC.

toxic pesticides; it's about the way you view nature and how you work with those who manage the land most intimately.

Environmentally Friendly Packaging

Packaging food involves much more than consumers realize. Our original (pre-sustainability program) packaging system included several components: first, the wrapper—a two-component system to keep moisture in, oxygen out, and the food clean; second, a paperboard caddy to hold bars, and a master case for shipping. These master cases got strapped to pallets with stretch-wrap and put into trucks. It's a huge system, all of which is basically invisible to the consumer, except the wrapper.

Our long-term goal is to make all packaging components more environmentally sound, and we're moving in that direction one concrete step at a time. Currently no recyclable wrapper offers the product protection that we need. The packaging industry is working on this, and we follow their research carefully. However, we redesigned the caddy in 2001 to get rid of the shrink-wrap, saving us $450,000 a year and eliminating enough of that non-biodegradable product to wrap the state of Texas. We took another step to green up our caddies in 2002 when Kevin Gnusti, product coordinator, found the right mix of materials to produce the ten million caddies we use each year out of 100 percent recycled (50 percent post-consumer) non-chlorine-bleached paperboard. This conversion saved us $50,000 annually, as well as 3.3 million gallons of water, seventy-five hundred trees, and enough energy for thirty-nine homes. We also avoid producing toxic chemicals like cancer-causing dioxins when we use paper that eliminates chlorine from the production process.

Greening the Office

In 2001, we started an environmental audit to identify ineffi-
ciencies in our use of energy, assess our overall waste output,
and explore ways of reducing, reusing, and recycling materials.
Office "green-up" initiatives include a switch to 100 percent
post-consumer recycled paper, desk-side recycling bins, and
bicycles for employees to use during work hours. StopWaste
helped us improve office energy efficiency and expand our recycling program; we collect compost, and we can now recycle
nonrigid plastic for our employees (like dry cleaning bags),
something not possible from home. We emphasize the reduction
of waste, as well as recycling. Employees use GOOS (good on
one side) paper to print whenever possible. Our warehouse
manager, Chris Tomsha, also collects used clothing in good condition to distribute through Mrs. Green's, a local nonprofit that
addresses the needs of inner-city children; we recycled 2,100
pounds of clothes in 2003.

Our in-house Internal Design Group wanted to use recycled
paper for all our outsourced printing. Mary Hudson found New
Leaf Paper in San Francisco, and New Leaf helped us find certified green printers. When we learned that cotton is one of the
most pesticide-intensive crops, we started using 100 percent
organic cotton T-shirts for all our promotional needs. We purchase about sixteen thousand organic cotton T-shirts annually
and avoid the use of five thousand pounds of agricultural chemicals in cotton production.

The "eco-posse," a volunteer group of employees from different
departments, helps to keep environmental efforts front and

THE STORY OF CLIF BAR, INC.

center. These efforts not only reduce waste, they support suppliers that use greener practices.

Clif Bar uses its economic power to affect the supply chain; we're a small part of creating a greener economy.

Our Fight Against Global Warming—
Clif Bar Tilts Toward Wind Mills

Clif's manufacturing, office, and other business practices (like travel) rely on fossil fuels that release carbon dioxide, the main greenhouse gas contributing to climate change, into the atmosphere. Elysa wanted us to do something to reduce our contribution to global warming. She proposed offsetting the carbon dioxide generated by our business with investments in wind energy. After a lively discussion around the office, during which Elysa faced tough questions, we started the Green Power Program and partnered with Native Energy to invest in the first Native American–owned wind farm. In 2002, we purchased enough wind energy credits to offset the carbon dioxide emissions generated by our office, manufacturing, and travel: 3.6 million pounds of carbon dioxide, the equivalent of removing 250 SUVs from the road for one year. We expanded the program in 2003 to include a tree-planting program to offset global warming pollution generated by employee commutes.

Every effort we make to reduce our environmental impact also reduces our contribution to global warming. When we converted seven million pounds of ingredients to organic, we decreased carbon dioxide emissions too. Organic farming, on average, uses 50 percent as much fossil fuel as conventional farming, produces less than a third the greenhouse gases, and builds up organic matter in the soil. Recycled paper and other office materials also take less energy to manufacture and reduce waste sent to landfills, thus generating less methane, another greenhouse gas. We realize that our company will continue to contribute to global warming as long as our economy depends on fossil fuels. In the meantime, buying green power, supporting organic agriculture, planting trees, and reducing waste are ways to offset carbon dioxide emissions.

Partners in Sustainability

A commitment to sustainability has to extend beyond our own practices. That's another reason that we partner with groups that share our vision for a healthier, more sustainable world. I've already talked about TBCF, whose mission is to identify and eliminate the environmental causes of breast cancer. Let me just add that TBCF has raised our consciousness, as individuals and as a company, about the plethora of toxic chemicals in our air, water, and food to which we're exposed every day—

what TBCF terms the preventable causes of breast cancer. Another Clif partner, the Children's Environmental Health Coalition, researches, educates, and advocates about protecting children from environmental health hazards. We also partner with Co-op America to encourage companies and individuals to use their economic power to build a healthier, greener economy. Our list of partners also includes Leave No Trace, The Access Fund, Pesticide Action Network, GreenTreks, The Food Alliance, The Circle of Life Foundation, The Waterkeeper Alliance, and the Organic Farming Research Foundation.

We generally provide financial support, product, and promotional materials for partners' events. We bring visibility to our partner organizations through our Web site, events, and packaging. Our field representatives also support environmental activities in their local areas, such as beach clean-ups in the Los Angeles area and the "Don't Mess with Texas" clean-up campaign. Clif people believe passionately in our company's journey toward sustainability. We are honored to partner with numerous organizations dedicated to the well-being of people and our planet.

Learning from and Encouraging Others

I learned, and keep learning, from other companies and business leaders. Patagonia initiated an environmental review of the company in 1991, changed its practices, and significantly reduced the environmental impact of its clothing production. Stonyfield Farm carefully monitors its environmental impact and encourages organic dairy farming. Organic Valley, the largest farmer-owned organic cooperative in the United States (with more than six hundred farmer members), is committed to sustaining family farms while producing healthy, organic food. New Leaf Paper makes recycled paper that saves trees, water, energy, and greenhouse gases in the process. Fetzer Vineyards is the largest California grower of organic wine grapes, setting a compelling example for the California wine industry.

It wasn't until we'd been around ten years that we converted to organic ingredients. Clif Bar Inc. shows that companies can learn and change. We've found that sustainability makes economic as well as environmental sense. Every time you reduce waste, you lessen your impact on the environment and you can save money.

Just as we follow in the steps of companies we admire, we hope to encourage others to adopt environmentally sound practices. Bruce, our attorney, watched Clif's sustainability program flourish. In the fall of 2002, he turned to me as we walked the streets of a picturesque village in Ireland and said, "I've been thinking this entire trip about how much paper a law office uses every year: hundreds of thousands of sheets of paper, printed on one side. Law offices need to become green." He returned to Oakland and convinced his law partners to adopt environmental sustainability as a company goal. His firm, Wendel, Rosen, Black & Dean, became the country's first green-certified law office. Tulip Graphics produces many of our brochures, posters, and newsletters. It printed our first in-house sustainability newsletter in 2001 using 100 percent post-consumer recycled paper for a high-quality product—a first for both of us. Not only did its people learn how to use this recycled paper well, they've embraced the vision of sustainability, expanded their collaboration with New Leaf Paper, and the company will soon be a green-certified printer. We're excited about the surprising ways that a commitment to sustainability influences other businesses.

Companies have tremendous economic power to promote products, services, and practices that benefit the environment. Do we treat the environment as a "silent stakeholder; a party to which the company is wholly accountable," as Batstone writes, or do we soil our own stream?

➤ STEWARDING THE CLIF ECOSYSTEM

The Clif ecosystem consists of five parts: sustaining our brands, business, people, community, and planet. Each aspiration is important in and of itself, yet the component parts interact, similar to an ecosystem in the natural world. What happens in one area affects other areas. We saw how that worked during 2003. We didn't sustain our brand well enough and that had an effect on our business, which in turn had an effect on morale. In an ecosystem everything is interdependent.

A certain number of human beings will probably survive no matter what destruction we wreak on the global ecosystem, even if they end up surviving in a world that looks like something out of *Mad Max* or *The Matrix.* Clif Bar Inc. might very well *survive* if we brought in outside investors or went public or sold to a big company, even if the employees ended up working for a company that never served a single weenie or martini, never pounded a single nail in a Habitat for Humanity house. Our brands could probably *survive,* even if they ended up nonorganic shells of their former selves. But survival is not the point. Human communities and cultures should *thrive,* and ecosystem health, biodiversity, and some degree of social equity are prerequisites for human thriving. Clif's incredible people, community service, environmental initiative, wellness program, and grassroots marketing are prerequisites for the company to survive and thrive.

I ride my bike because I love to be on my bike. I don't ride just to get to the finish line; what happens on the bike makes the experience. I love white-road journeys. I thrill at the high mountain peaks, the feel of the pedals and gears, the picturesque villages, the shared loaves of bread, the physical challenges, the being in a space where I can think clearly and listen to my heart.

CLIF COULD SURVIVE ON THE RED ROAD. WOULD WE THRIVE? I DOUBT IT. CLIF BAR INC. RIDES THE WHITE ROADS. WE EXIST TO THRIVE, NOT MERELY SURVIVE.

RAISING THE BAR

THE STORY OF CLIF BAR, INC.

CHAPTER 8

MOMENTS OF MAGIC

I started playing piano at the age of four, maybe because my mom taught the instrument. I loved the piano, but as I progressed it got more and more difficult to read piano music, and I started to rely on my ear to play. Later I understood why reading all that multi-chord, two-handed music was so difficult: I'm dyslexic. In the fifth grade, I decided that trumpet would be my instrument, maybe because trumpet music involves reading one line of notes at a time. Sight-reading was never easy for me (still isn't), but my disability gave me two gifts: a good ear and near perfect pitch.

When I was in the seventh grade, my mom signed me up for trumpet lessons with Larry Jonutz, a well-known jazz horn player. Jonutz played in Cold Blood, a Bay Area band that had made its mark on the national scene playing a funk sound similar to Tower of Power and Blood, Sweat and Tears. One day, after I'd been studying "regular" music with Larry for a while, he said, "I'm going to give you five notes to play while I play

GARY SOLOING WITH LEDISI. —PAUL MCKENZIE

chords in the background. Only play those five notes, and make them sound *good*." That's how I was introduced to jazz improvisation. After that, Larry took me deeper and deeper into the world of jazz. He said you have to listen to jazz to play jazz and I listened and listened. He loaned me albums, and once a month he took me to the Great American Music Hall to see the great jazz artists of the time perform. I heard everybody: Freddie Hubbard, Buddy Rich, Maynard Ferguson, Stan Kenton, Don Ellis, and the list goes on. Usually I was the only kid in the club—a seventh grader in a room filled with cigarette smoke and clinking glasses—all of us grooving to great jazz.

If that wasn't exciting enough, Cold Blood let me sit in on some instrumental rehearsals. There I'd be in a garage complete with Hammond B3 organ, black lights, and a bunch of cool dudes jamming. It was junior-high heaven. They'd look at me and say, "Okay, man, it's time to solo. You're on." I'd pick up my horn and play. I knew that I didn't sound that good, but what a thrill to be playing with these world-class musicians.

My love for all music, and especially for jazz, grew from these heady beginnings. I played my horn through high school in small combos, jazz groups, and bands, and toured with a jazz ensemble. I went to San Jose State University to pursue a music degree but decided after a week that the touring life of smoky clubs in major cities didn't suit my outdoorsy nature. I majored in business instead, but I continued to play music through my college years, performing with small horn bands and big band ensembles. In my late twenties I was too busy climbing and traveling around the world to play my horn much, but I picked it up again in my thirties and played around the

San Francisco Bay Area in small clubs and with the Island
City Big Band. I've been fortunate to play backup behind six or
seven wonderful female jazz singers, my favorite gig. I didn't
make a career out of making music, yet from its inception Clif
Bar has reflected lessons I learned from jazz.

> **ENSEMBLE PLAYING**

Playing my horn alone gets old; I can't create a complete sound.
I need to play with other people, but I have trouble playing with
musicians who aren't intense about their craft. If people aren't
grooving, if they aren't together and listening to me and to each
other, if it isn't happening, I can barely play. But, when *it* happens, something clicks and I perform beyond what I think is
possible.

The *beyond* experience happened for me again (as it had countless times before) in the fall of 2003 when I played with Ledisi,
a great jazz and soul performer, at the concert celebrating the
opening of the Clif Bar Performing Arts Theater. Leslie Abra-
ham from Clif introduced me to Ledisi as the owner of Clif Bar
and told her I played the trumpet. I had hoped to sit in for a
tune or two even though I hadn't performed more than a couple
of times over the last few years. Ledisi said, "My sax player
didn't show up; you're sitting in." No audition. Nothing! I started
out slow but soon felt the drummer listening to what I was
doing. I sustained notes and experimented with rhythms; the
drummer and the organ player challenged me to push it even
further. I felt as if I were out of my body. It was truly an ensemble coming together, creating magic. People who play know
these magic moments, which happen only when a special group

RAISING THE BAR

THE STORY OF CLIF BAR, INC.

of people create their own chemistry. Such moments are central in the history of jazz. When I listen to Miles Davis, Lee Morgan, John Coltrane, Bill Evans, Wes Montgomery, Betty Carter, and other jazz greats, I feel traces of that kind of magic.

ENSEMBLE PLAYING BROUGHT CLIF BAR TO LIFE. When I had the idea to create an energy bar I went to a great "musician," my mom. She and I played a duet with tastes, textures, and recipes. After six months improvising together in her kitchen we came up with the prototype for the Clif Bar. I couldn't have done it in isolation. I knew Doug Gilmour's talent, just as Miles Davis knew Coltrane's. During that magic moment over lunch described in Chapter Two, Doug and I played a duet that led to the first Clif Bar package. A group of Clif people, including Dean Mayer and his PR team, wanted to create something out of the ordinary and they ended up developing LunaFest, a film festival by, for, and about women. But they didn't enter the room with the idea of starting a film festival. They simply sat down together and let their creative juices flow; they played together. They thought about how women artists, directors, and filmmakers are underrepresented in the film industry, and they thought about how many lives are touched by breast cancer. They proposed a way to provide more opportunities for women to show their films while raising funds and consciousness about breast cancer. In 2003, LunaFest traveled to fifty

venues and it keeps growing. Even this book is a duet played by
Lois and me.

**I don't believe that creative work, whether in jazz or in busi-
ness, happens in isolation. It takes the energy of an ensemble
to make magic.**

➤ LISTENING

If your background player just bangs out the chords in a predictable manner, you don't have to listen that carefully—you
can simply play what you think will sound cool against this set
model. If they start mixing it up, though, you had better be
paying attention. Sometimes I take fellow musicians to a new
place, other times they take me for a ride. It's hard to explain.
Maybe I want to sustain a note for a long time, play around
rhythmically. If the other musicians are listening to me, they
will go with it. You can play around like that in improvisation,
even if it falls outside the model of the standard twelve-chord
progression, if you're listening.

At Clif Bar we have to listen carefully to what's happening, both
internally within the company and externally. Let's say we create a new bar, the person in charge plays a solo, but must listen
carefully to Finance, and Finance has to listen to the person in

charge. Community Service, if it's listening, may find a cause that fits the music from the product. All over the company, people with different skills must listen carefully to each other as they work together. Our Research and Development people, for example, come from different backgrounds: some are classically trained food scientists, one began as a rock climber, and another is a chef. They play together in a restaurant-style kitchen rather than in a traditional food lab. A certain kind of chemistry occurs when people from different backgrounds, like our R&D team, listen attentively to each other as they work.

As an entrepreneur, I listen carefully to my gut, intuition, creativity, whatever you call it. I also listen carefully to the various types of music played by other companies. Over the years when Miles heard accolades claiming that he was *the* jazz musician of the century, he responded by saying, "No, Louis Armstrong was." And who would Armstrong have said was the greatest? Probably not Armstrong. The point: jazz didn't just happen; musicians listening attentively to other musicians created it over time. I listened carefully to what happened with Ben & Jerry's, Odwalla, Balance Bar, and other companies. Patagonia turned me on with its music. Companies, like bands, have their own sound.

A great business, like great jazz, depends on careful listening.

➤ SPACES AND SILENCES—PUSHING THE EDGE

I thought I listened to everything: rock, classical music, soul, blues, high-powered big bands, funk bands, great trumpet players, piano players. Name the jazz musician and I listened, or so I thought. Then I heard Miles Davis. I was thrown off; what he played was so cool, simultaneously so simple and so complex. It was a new sound to me and to the world. I loved Dizzy Gillespie, Freddie Hubbard, Charlie Parker, and other bebop greats. It had always amazed me how many notes bebop players could play in twelve bars: they played fast and they played until it seemed they couldn't breathe. People loved it. Then along came Miles Davis. When he soloed, Miles might hold a note for a long time, then stop and not make a sound for four counts. He created space: yet within the space, even though he wasn't playing music, was music. Sometimes the silence itself was the music, sometimes his background musicians created music. Miles forced other players to use the space left by the soloist. Entrepreneurs and business owners can learn a lot from Miles and from the music of silence and space. I want to lead and also step aside, creating space within the company for other people to take solos and for the background musicians to create.

Miles used space and silence to create tension, an edge. Good musicians know how to create and release tension; a great jazz solo is one that continually creates and releases, creates and releases. I believe a good advertisement creates and releases a similar tension. Doug and I have always tried to shape ads with an edge. The Clif Bar ad (created by Doug, Sheryl, and me) featuring my dad and me is one example. The ad tells part of the history of Clif Bar as told by my dad. He didn't approve of my lifestyle, we experienced some tension between us, and then I went and named the bar I developed after him! This authentic story both created and released tension and formed the core of our 2003 advertising campaign.

CLIF AD—GARY AND DAD.
—PHOTO: STUART SCHWARTZ; AD CREATED BY DOUG GILMOUR,
GARY ERICKSON, SHERYL O'LOUGHLIN

In 1990, my son turned 33 and moved into a garage.

He didn't have a regular job-job.
Oh sure, he had time to race his bike.
And rock climb. And play that trumpet in jazz
bars until who knows when. And you can be
sure nothing got in the way of those countless
treks. Places I'd never heard of.
We've had our moments through the years.
But all this (pause) really gets a father wondering.

Then he names Clif Bar® after me.

I worry too much. — Clifford Erickson/father of owner

For more of the Clif Bar story, visit www.clifbar.com (800) CLIF BAR

Every flavor made with
certified organic ingredients

I love the way jazz improvisation pushes the edge; that's what
makes it so beautiful to me. Miles recorded *Kind of Blue,*
played it for a year or two, and then was done with it. People
wanted him to keep playing *Kind of Blue* until the day he died,
but he moved on to the next thing. Miles relied on constant
reinvention, rather than on a formula that was guaranteed to
be popular and sell (I won't name the performers who come
to mind that rely on a formula). Maybe Miles never sold as
many albums as the formulaic performers, but he followed his
heart and awakened listeners to a sound they didn't even know
was possible. He gave his listeners, including me, "ah hah"
moments.

We try to push, to play on the edge at Clif Bar. The Mojo Bar
for example, broke the mold of sweet energy and nutrition bars,
and I wanted to push further by introducing edgy flavors. The
first Mojo Bar flavors I created were Thai Peanut, using lemon-
grass, Thai peanut sauce, and dried vegetables. We tried bar-
beque and spicy peanut flavors, and I insisted on producing
Curry Cashew because I wanted to push the limits, even though
people told me they never imagined a curry nutrition bar. Those
initial flavors developed a cult following, unfortunately they
never sold enough to be sustainable. Those flavors didn't take
off, but I still believe that being willing to push the limits, even
if you fear that your listeners or consumers can't handle it, is a

RAISING THE BAR

THE STORY OF CLIF BAR, INC.

good thing. Like a good improv combo we continually reinvent ourselves, hoping to offer people edgy food experiences.

➤ IMPERFECTION

Jazz isn't about being perfect. When my high school jazz ensemble tuned up, we all tried our B flats or concert As. We'd joke that our tuning was "close enough for jazz," meaning it wasn't absolute perfection but would fly. Of course we wanted to be as close to perfect as possible, but we also knew that jazz gave us the freedom to be less than perfect. In junior college, my harmony teacher asked us if any imperfect notes existed in jazz improvisation. A classmate answered, "No. It is how long you hold the note that might be imperfect." He meant that it is all right to make a mistake because you can usually get out of it by moving into another note quickly. You can play a note, or even a few notes, that don't fit as long as you come back and resolve your mistake. The imperfection becomes part of the music, if you don't hold on too long. Similarly, the nature of our business is to explore and improvise. You aren't doing your job right if you aren't making mistakes. The true mistake occurs when you hold on to the wrong note for too long, and we have done this at Clif Bar. We've held on to mistakes for so long (you've read about some of these errors in this book) that it actually hurt the business.

Let's go back to where I was sitting on stage with Ledisi getting ready to play a solo. I knew that I might screw up in front of hundreds of people, including Clif employees. It was hard for me to get going, and I made mistakes on my first solo. I thought, "I could look like a complete fool up here," but I was willing to warm up, make a few mistakes, and take the risk.

Entrepreneurs and entrepreneurial companies, by definition, make mistakes. It's part of the music.

> **ON STAGE**

Had I been able to rehearse with Ledisi and her band Anibade, I would have hung back to see how I fit in with the other musicians. The night of the concert I didn't have that luxury. I was performing before an audience of two hundred people, including my employees and friends. I felt a lot of pressure. It was the real deal and I had to perform. Some of our most magic sessions at Clif Bar occurred under pressure. Luna Glow, our low-carbohydrate bar, was produced under intense pressure. The rest of Clif Bar watched as different ensembles created a bar and designed a new package in record time. The pressure pushed these Clif musicians to a new level of performance. Magic happened.

RAISING
THE BAR

THE STORY OF CLIF BAR, INC.

I believe so much in the whole magic of performance that when we added additional warehouse space, I knew that I wanted to build a world-class performing arts theater. I didn't have all the reasons figured out, but in my gut I hoped that if we built a Clif Field of Dreams, then they would come. I wanted a miniature version of Yoshi's, the Bay Area's hottest jazz club. In September 2003, the Clif Bar Performing Arts Theater was completed. It boasts a world-class stage, thirty-two microphones, a twenty-five by twenty-five-foot screen, and surround sound. The sound system is good enough to make live recordings. Our first event was the debut of the Luna Chix film by Nicole Hahn, our in-house filmmaker. Our second event featured Tyler Hamilton, the cyclist who placed fourth in the Tour de France in 2003 while riding with a broken collarbone; it sold out to three hundred people within three days. To celebrate the theater's opening, we converted the space into a nightclub and hosted Ledisi.

We see endless possibilities for the Clif Bar Performing Arts Theater, including literary readings, sports symposia, live radio shows, music concerts, film screenings, environmental workshops, and theater performances. Clif Bar cast, directed, and performed the play *Vagina Monologues.* Every Thursday night employees play rock and bluegrass in a jam session on the Clif stage. In retrospect it makes sense that Clif built a performing arts space: Clif people are performers, and creating magic for ourselves and for our community is central to our company.

➤ MAGIC MOMENTS

I've never been a full-time professional musician, but I know the magic feeling of losing myself while playing jazz. I'll be

CLIF PERFORMING ARTS THEATER.
—PAUL McKENZIE

TYLER HAMILTON INTERVIEW.

listening intently to the other musicians, playing, performing in front of a crowd, and at some point all I see are the notes, all I hear are the notes. When I get in that groove, I literally forget that there are people out there. I feel transported, as if I'm playing outside of myself. I wonder: "How is this happening? How are these notes coming out of my horn?" Being lost in a business moment occurs during those live sessions when you gather the right people together, when everyone is open, and not pushing particular agendas. It's important to bring your talents, skills, and ideas to a meeting, but it's also important to be willing to go to a place you may not have imagined before entering the room.

One of the most magical processes in the history of jazz was the creation of the album *Kind of Blue*. The musicians were accustomed to playing bebop and showed up at the studio with some music already scripted and other tunes written on notepads. Miles said he didn't want to write the music because he "wanted a lot of spontaneity in the playing." The musicians weren't used to playing the new sound Miles had in mind, but got into the groove during the two long sessions that lasted two days. Fortunately for us, they taped the entire session so we can hear their ongoing banter. The timing, getting the right people together, and having a leader (Miles) with a vision, resulted in a magic session and one of the all-time great jazz albums. Magic doesn't always happen; you may have the wrong people, you may not be listening to each other, or it doesn't happen for reasons you can't control or understand. But, other times, bam, *it just happens!* I've seen magic happen at Clif Bar over the years. It doesn't happen just around marketing a product or brand, or creating a new taste or an advertisement. It can happen anytime, anywhere, for any reason. The 2080 Program started when the right players got together at the right moment and played the music: Clif benefited from their creativity by receiving a community service program.

During the summer of 2001, I spent time at the beach with my eight-year-old daughter Lydia. I watched her run, splash, dig, jump; what energy she had! What desire to move her body! I wondered what opportunities would be available to her as she grew. I knew that possibilities for women in sports remain limited and that Title IX is under threat. I thought about how the women's professional soccer league had been disbanded, how only professional women's basketball was still around. Watching Lydia play inspired me. I decided that I wanted Clif to sponsor a women's professional mountain bike team. I had no idea how to go about sponsoring the team, but I knew I had to do it. (Don't worry, I won't pressure Lydia to become a mountain bike racer.) Paul McKenzie, Dave McLaughlin, and I joined forces to make my dream come true. We encountered one magic moment after another as we began to form a team. First, we

RAISING THE BAR

THE STORY OF CLIF BAR, INC.

LUNA CHIX.

—MALCOLM FEARON

called Alison Dunlap, the current world champion women's mountain bike racer, Marla Streb, a world-class downhill racer and author of *Downhill Gravity Goddess,* and Gina Hall, a cyclocross and mountain bike racer. They signed on and the Luna Women's Mountain Bike Team—"Luna Chix"—was born. The team later included Shonny Vanlandingham, Kathy Pruitt, Katerina Hanusova, and Kelli Emmet. We told the bike industry what we were doing and were shocked by the overwhelmingly positive response. Everyone wanted to be part of the team: bicycle companies (we choose the best, Santa Cruz Bicycles), clothing and shoe companies, you name it. LUNA CHIX TOOK THE WORLD BY STORM; *Mountain Bike* magazine called the creation of the team "one of the most significant new efforts the racing community has seen in years." To my knowledge, Luna Chix is the only professional sports team where women athletes make comparable salaries to men athletes. Once the team was up and running, Paul took over as the lead musician of a team ensemble that plays with incredible synergy. Many people in the bike industry have told me that they've never seen a better-run team than Luna Chix. All the people involved—the mechanics, team managers, directors, PR and advertising team, as well as the cyclists—are incredibly approachable, super nice, and high-performing.

Luna Chix, like the other great athletes we sponsor, contributes to Clif excitement. We added the Luna Ambassadors to the mix. The Luna Ambassadors are groups of women who race at the amateur level. They offer mountain bike clinics (alongside our professional racers) to bring more women into the sport. The Luna Chix team, magical in and of itself, added magic to

RAISING THE BAR

THE STORY OF CLIF BAR, INC.

magic and became about more than mountain biking. Luna
Chix is also about empowering women in sports.

Countless other examples of Clif magic exist. Many Clif employees run marathons. A lot of people hope to make a certain time,
but they're on their own trying to accomplish that aim. A group
decided to create the Clif Pace Team as a way to support the
specific goals of individual runners or groups of runners. The
team matches members to runners, and the Pace Team accom-
panies people for an entire race: If you want to run a marathon
in three hours and fifteen minutes you run with Kenny Souza;
If you want to run in three hours and thirty minutes you run
with someone else, and so on. Kenny recently ran a three-hour,
fifteen-minute marathon with a group of twenty people.
Throughout the race he kept asking each of them how they
were doing, if they needed water or Clif Shot. The Clif Pace
Team emerged from a magic moment at Clif Bar, and it now
provides magic for others.

> IMPROVISATION: FREEDOM AND FORM

Playing jazz trumpet taught me the importance of discipline
and training. Without discipline and long hours of practice
there's no music. Training sets the groundwork, but to play jazz
you need to be in the moment. You improvise. I don't practice
the licks or riffs of an improvisational piece. I don't play them
until the music is happening. But that doesn't mean that I get
up there without any preparation. I have to be in shape. I have
to practice my scales, understand music, listen to a lot of musicians, and have a decent horn. Jazz has a structure: you can't be
so off and weird that no one understands what you're doing.

Improvisation offers a special freedom within the structure of jazz music. Clif employees who've worked at large companies tell us that Clif offers more freedom to express opinions, to experiment, and to be creative. I think we can have this improvisational sort of freedom in our business because the shareholders don't force the bottom line. That allows us to explore a variety of directions. I hope that we give our employees the freedom to express, to improvise, and to take a solo now and then.

Form exists in jazz, yet improvisation guarantees innovation and surprises. We want to see where our new music takes us.

> JAZZ—THE SOUL OF OUR BUSINESS MODEL

Moments of magic, ensemble playing, improvisation, and freedom are at the heart of our company. The guidelines I've developed for a sustainable business model are only guidelines; they aren't the music.

The business model is like a written score; but everything depends on how you play the music. Can the musicians, whether in jazz or business, breathe life into the written score? Jazz takes musicians, or companies, to surprising places, to places beyond their expectations.

The core is jazz: the freedom to improvise in the creation of beautiful things, products, and people.

RAISING

THE BAR

THE STORY OF CLIF BAR, INC.

THE NATURE OF THINGS

I wrote *Raising the Bar* three years ago. A lot has changed since then: we changed our name from Clif Bar Inc. to Clif Bar & Company; Kit devotes more energy to the company; and, after two hard years in 2003 and 2004, we experienced a record year in 2005. I fulfilled a personal dream and competed in Ironman Canada and Ironman Florida in 2005. Last week another dream came true: Bank of America returned our stock certificates. We officially own the company!

Big changes no doubt, but none that alter the substance of *Raising the Bar*. I didn't know it at the time, but my walk around the block exposed *the nature of things* to me; it revealed what I wanted in a partnership, in the company, in my life, and in my marriage. I've thought a lot about nature's ecosystems and how these apply to our business and my life. Today, more than ever, I believe that ecosystems, individuals, communities, and businesses thrive when we identify and then attend to the intricate nature of things.

GARY IN IRONMAN FLORIDA TRIATHLON.
—WWW.ASIPHOTO.COM

RAISING
THE BAR

THE STORY OF CLIF BAR, INC.

> LETTING GO

One big change: I am no longer CEO of the company I founded. As I wrote in Chapter Six, planning for succession is one of the most difficult tasks entrepreneurs are called upon to do. Many find it impossible to let go and allow someone else to run the day-to-day operations of their companies. It makes sense; who wants to hand over their passion, their dream, their baby to someone else?

I started Clif Bar, didn't sell, and stuck with it through the growing pains described in this book. Yet I sensed that I had lost my ability to manage the business effectively on a daily basis. I came to feel that the intricacies of running multiple departments surpassed my skill level. I also found it was difficult to avoid the "brutal facts" syndrome. Jim Collins in *Good to Great* writes that CEOs need to know the brutal facts about their own company, but no one likes to disappoint a founder and owner. Who, after all, wants to bring bad news to the top? When it came down to it, I realized that the entrepreneur-owner-CEO model no longer worked for the company or for me. As I made plans for a succession, I knew that I didn't want to hire a CEO off the street. I needed someone to succeed me who possessed the right skills *and* the passion *and* the vision that make Clif special. I found such a person in Sheryl O'Loughlin, who joined Clif in 1998 as our first brand manager. Sheryl developed a management team that keeps the values, culture, and vision of Clif thriving, and Kit and I trust her, and them, completely. We've remained involved and work with Sheryl on a weekly basis. Although as owners we hold ultimate control, we're thrilled that Sheryl and the management team are taking the company in a direction that fits our vision and boasts her unique stamp.

> PLAY YOUR OWN GAME

I wrote in Chapter Five that our coach, Frank Mangiola, always told our soccer team to "keep playing your own game." One of the biggest recent mistakes at Clif happened because I didn't heed Mangiola's advice. At a certain point we began to get pressure from retailers to develop a low-carb product. The pressure grew exponentially. Retailers and distributors told us, "Don't show us anything unless you have a low-carb product." One of our lenders, Allied Capital, also pressured us. We yielded and produced Glow, a product that came and went as fast as the low-carb fad. We lost money, took product back, discarded inventory, and ended up wondering, "What happened?"

We learned from our mistake. We had listened to other people's judgments about what niche to fill. Although we thought that low-carb reflected a sustainable trend, we have a vision—and a big part of that vision is to move toward organic. Yet we created this product that felt like a synthetic knockoff of other low-carb bars, a product that didn't meet the usual Clif standards for taste and nutrition. Employees thought the Glow decision put us on the red road; it seemed to be about making money rather than staying true to our game. We learned, once again, to listen to ourselves rather than to external voices. We can't go against our corporate DNA.

> GROWING ORGANICALLY

Today our products better reflect the Clif nature of things; we are staying true to our roots and to our vision of going organic. Clif Bar, Luna, Mojo, and Clif Shot now contain 70 percent certified organic ingredients. Z Bar and Shot Blocks contain 95 percent organic ingredients. Our new products fit this vision: the Luna Sunrise breakfast bar boasts 70 percent certified organic ingredients and the Nectar fruit and nut bar, 95 percent. We developed Clif Shot Electrolyte Replacement Drink, the first powdered sports drink that is certified organic, at 92 percent. Clif Shot Recovery Drink, although not certified, contains 76 percent organic ingredients.

We strive to create the most natural and organic products possible, and in 2005 we created more new products than at any point in Clif history. Sustainability is about more than creating organic products, however. Clif undertook an eco-assessment of our entire supply chain; we're measuring the energy used from the farm to the baker to the distributor to the consumer. Following this in-depth eco-audit, we are working to reduce our impact as quickly as possible. In the meantime we are moving toward zero waste at our headquarters. Currently, through recycling and composting, we divert 80 percent of our waste from the landfill. Our biodiesel tour, now in its third year, shares ideas about how to address global warming, and we encourage our event partners to move toward climate neutrality. For example, we helped the Tour de California cycling race, a U.S. version of the Tour de France, to become the first cycling event to go green. We link social equity with efforts to reduce our ecological footprint; our supplier code of conduct addresses fairness to workers.

Morale at the business is good because people embrace the products we make and our journey toward sustainability. Sixty-five people worked at Clif Bar when we almost sold in 2000; by 2006 that number has grown to 160. We had *mojo* at the end of 2000, when we turned the company around, but the question was, "Can we keep it with so many people?" We found out that you can when you stick to your core values. We work at maintaining authenticity, innovation, and social integrity. We strive to support the communities we sell in, as well as the environment.

> **DISCIPLINED ENTREPRENEURIAL PLAYERS:**
> **THE CLIMBER'S BALANCE**

I learned the hard way that climbers need at least three points of contact at all times when on ice or rock (see my tale "On Ice, Shaken but Not Stirred" in Chapter Five). Why? It's the only way to balance. Just one point, you will fall. Two points, you can hang on for a bit, but not for long. Three points, you are rock solid. Sheryl adapted this climbing truth to our business. One day, while Kit, Sheryl, and I were talking, we asked ourselves, "What kind of culture do we want to create at Clif Bar?" We came up with three words that we thought best described Clif culture: *Disciplined (D), Entrepreneurial (E),* and *Playful (P).* Just as climbers do, Clif needs three points of contact (D.E.P.) to stay balanced.

I'm not a very disciplined entrepreneur. I'm not big on details and typically go for getting things done by hook or by crook. Working with a guy like me proved difficult for Sheryl. Early in our relationship we talked over a beer in a local pub about the tension between us. I was way E, she was way D, and it drove us crazy. I feared that Clif would become too corporate and bureaucratic. She thought I didn't have a clue about how to run a business. As she says, "We don't want to just get lucky, we want to be prepared and protected." Discipline gives a company the advantage of learning from mistakes, turning that learning into processes, and turning the energy unleashed by efficient operations into more entrepreneurial activities. Even an E guy like me recognizes the big payoff we gain from discipline.

Discipline is important; however, Clif Bar came into being because of an entrepreneurial mind-set that favors creativity, following the white roads, experimentation, risk taking, looking for the next "ah ha." A small company like ours can't outspend the big guys, but we can outcreate them. What got us here is our ability to play: I played in the kitchen, on my bike, with my horn. Playing also means collaborating. Can employees catch the entrepreneurial spirit when their capital isn't on the line; can they feel the risk of being an entrepreneur? I believe that entrepreneurial breakthroughs happen at Clif when employees playfully collaborate together, creating and imagining new processes and solutions. The power of the group balances the D with the E; dancing the tension between discipline and entrepreneurship is the answer. Discipline. Entrepreneurial mindset. Creative play. With these three points of balance, any company can go from good to great.

➤ OUR BUSINESS MODEL WORKS!

Chapter Seven began with the question, "What return on investment do I get from a white-road journey or first ascent?" Kit and I asked ourselves what we wanted from Clif Bar and realized that our return on investment boiled down to five aspirations: sustaining our brands, our business, our people, our community, and our planet. We developed a business model based on these five aspirations and see it as a grand experiment in redefining shareholder value. When I wrote the book, the model was in its infancy. Before, like most companies, we focused primarily on using EBIDTA (earnings before interest, depreciation, taxes, and amortization) to measure our business success, or lack of it. We realized, as we developed our business model, that EBIDTA is only part of the equation. Now, in addition to EBIDTA, we make long- and short-term goals for each of the other four aspirations, using both qualitative and quantitative key performance indicators (KPIs) to measure our success. For *brands,* we measure the number of new products, retail distribution, and product quality; for *people,* the number of employees participating in Clif Bar University core courses, voluntary turnover, and morale; for *community,* community service hours as well as cash and product donations; and for *planet,* eco-assessment, our percentage of certified organic product, and the number of people trained in The Natural Step (a workshop on scientifically based principles to guide companies toward sustainability). Our KPIs measure each piece of the Clif ecosystem. I'll bet there aren't many VPs of finance that report the results of four other aspirations alongside the business numbers, like Rich does. We've learned that measuring a business with five bottom lines is doable.

I know our employees would be devastated if we hit our numbers but didn't meet our environmental and community service goals. Our business model makes us an even healthier business; the more we balance and progress in each of our five aspirations, the stronger we become as a company. Clif shows that a company that moves from bottom-line, red-road thinking to a stewardship model can thrive.

➤ PARTNERSHIP REVISITED

While on speaking tours after *Raising the Bar* was published, I saw that entrepreneurs were especially intrigued by the partnership described in the book. Numerous entrepreneurs spoke with me about their partnership issues; they feared their own "day of reckoning" would come, or worse, they worried about the effect on the company if the partnership did *not* dissolve. My recommendation was always, "Get a shareholder agreement." Like me, many had no agreements. What if one partner dies? Gets sick? Wants to leave the company? Wants to go left when you think you should go right? You need a way to resolve disagreements in a way that doesn't harm the company. People rush into partnerships on the strength of a handshake, and it can cost dearly.

For years I denied the nature of things in my own life, and instead I tried to convince Lisa to stay in the game and keep Clif as a privately held company. As we negotiated the buyout, I finally realized that the partnership needed to end, both for my own health and for the well-being of the company. I could

RAISING THE BAR

THE STORY OF CLIF BAR, INC.

KIT ON HER FIRST WHITE-ROAD TOUR IN THE DOLOMITES OF ITALY.
—GARY ERICKSON

no longer live in the fear and insecurity she brought to Clif. I realize now we should have terminated our partnership three years earlier, but I hadn't been paying close enough attention to my gut. When I finally figured out that I needed to dissolve this partnership, I experienced personal freedom, and I knew that Clif could now follow the white road.

> **KIT'S WELCOME MAT**

Kit was part of my life from the first year Clif existed. Techni-
cally she became a 50 percent owner of the business when she
married me. Yet, because of my dysfunctional relationship with
Lisa, she felt she faced a big No Trespassing sign when she
walked through the company door. She felt her involvement
and opinion didn't count. I handled the day-to-day managing of
the business and became the conduit for our collective vision.
After I ended the business partnership, Kit found natural ways
of becoming involved at Clif. The No Trespassing sign became a
Welcome mat. Kit told me, "If we had sold Clif Bar we would
have lost a great gift; now we can try to make a difference in the
world through our unique company."

Today she serves as a resource for the entire company; as an
owner she plays a fiduciary role that includes responsibilities
for annual budget and plan, long-term vision, business succession, and estate planning. With her direction, the LunaFest
team created a professional board, and together they have
turned LunaFest into a high-quality women's film festival; each
year the number and quality of the films shown has increased
dramatically, as has the press coverage. Kit steers and focuses
our community service aspiration. She has been instrumental
in formalizing our philanthropy through the Clif Bar Family
Foundation. One percent of all annual sales and people's time
go to a variety of charitable and nonprofit organizations.

Today, Kit gets to know our incredible employees over cup after
cup of delicious tea. And—last but not least—meetings with our
CEO include both owners. Now Kit and I shape Clif's direction

A NEW WHITE-ROAD ADVENTURE BEGINS.
—STUART SCHWARTZ

together. We want to keep the company through our lifetime and sustain our business, brand, people, community, and planet.

> BACK TO THE GARAGE

After writing *Raising the Bar,* I realized that I missed the garage. I missed being a hands-on entrepreneur. I missed creating new products and being the entrepreneurial guy. When Sheryl succeeded me as CEO, it gave Kit and me the opportunity to go back to the garage. We started Clif Bar Family Winery and Farm. Our products are wine and olive oil, but who knows where we will go from there. I do everything, just like in the old days at Clif. I put labels on bottles by hand, order supplies, write checks, develop products, make sales calls, and oversee production. And I'm having the time of my life!

From the beginning we wanted to go organic, but found it wasn't all that easy to find organic vineyards. After struggling to source enough organic for our new endeavors, Kit experienced her own epiphany, which quickly became a central vision for the business. Why not help small farms make the transition to organic? We now work with farmers who are on the fence, who may not know how to farm organically, or maybe haven't had compelling enough reasons to take the organic turn. We contract with them to buy grapes or olives, which allows them to take the first step. Within three years they can become certified. We're helping two small farms in Napa County, one grape and the other olive, to switch to organic farming. The vision for Clif Bar Family Winery and Farm clearly fits the nature of things for Kit and me. We support organic agriculture, family farms, artisan-handcrafted foods, locally grown ingredients, and careful food preparation with high-quality ingredients. Our products emphasize the value of food, wine, and companionship. We feel like we're riding together on a new white road, enjoying the scenery, sharing loaves of bread, and listening to our hearts.

RAISING
THE
BAR

THE STORY OF CLIF BAR, INC.

'92 CLIF BAR

'96 CLIF SHOT

'99 LUNA BAR

'02 CLIF MOJO

'04 CLIF BUILDER'S
CLIF ZBaR < for KIDS >

'05 CLIF NECTAR

'06 CLIF BAR FAMILY WINERY

CURRENT BRAND HISTORY

RESOURCES

Batstone, David. 2003. *Saving the Corporate Soul and (Who Knows?) Maybe Your Own: Eight Principles for Creating and Preserving Integrity and Profitability Without Selling Out.* San Francisco: Jossey-Bass.

Berry, Wendell. 1977. *The Unsettling of America: Culture and Agriculture.* New York: Avon Books.

Bossidy, Larry, and Ram Charan. 2002. *Execution: The Discipline of Getting Things Done.* New York: Crown Business.

Chappell, Tom. 1993. *The Soul of a Business: Managing for Profit and the Common Good.* New York: Bantam Books.

Cheverton, Richard E., Wilson, Bill and Vincent, Lanny. 2000. *The Maverick Way: Profiting from the Power of the Corporate Misfit.* La Palma, CA: Maverick Way Publishing.

Christensen, Clayton M., and Michael E. Raynor. 2003. *The Innovator's Solution: Creating and Sustaining Successful Growth.* Boston: Harvard Business School Press.

Cohen, Ben, and Jerry Greenfield. 1997. *Ben and Jerry's Double-Dip: Lead with Your Values and Make Money Too!* New York: Simon & Schuster.

Collins, Jim. 2001. *Good to Great: Why Some Companies Make the Leap . . . and Others Don't.* New York: HarperCollins.

De Geus, Arie. 1997. *The Living Company: Habits for Survival in a Turbulent Business Environment.* Boston: Harvard Business School Press.

Dolan, Paul. 2003. *True to our Roots: Fermenting a Business Revolution.* Princeton, NJ: Bloomberg Press.

Gladwell, Malcolm. 2000. *The Tipping Point: How Little Things Can Make a Big Difference.* New York: Little, Brown.

Hawken, Paul. 2000. *Natural Capitalism: Creating the Next Industrial Revolution*. Boston: Back Bay Books.

Hill, Julia. 2001. *The Legacy of Luna: The Story of a Tree, a Woman, and the Struggle to Save the Redwoods*. New York: HarperCollins.

Hollender, Jeffrey, and Stephen Fenichell. 2004. *What Matters Most: How a Small Group of Pioneers Is Teaching Social Responsibility to Big Business, and Why Big Business Is Listening*. New York: Basic Books.

Jensen, Rolf. 1999. *The Dream Society: How the Coming Shift from Information to Imagination Will Transform Your Business*. New York: McGraw-Hill.

Kahn, Ashley. 2000. *Kind of Blue: The Making of the Miles Davis Masterpiece*. New York: Da Capo Press.

Kauk, Ron. 2003. *Spirit of the Rock*. Layton, UT: Gibbs Smith.

Lazlo, Chris. 2003. *The Sustainable Company: How to Create Lasting Value Through Social and Environmental Performance*. Washington, DC: Island Press.

Lewis, David, and Darren Bridger. 2000. *The Soul of the New Consumer: Authenticity—What We Buy and Why in the New Economy*. London: Brealey.

Lipton, Mark. 2003. *Guiding Growth: How Vision Keeps Companies on Course*. Boston: Harvard Business School Press.

Marriner, Michael, and Nathan Gebhard. 2003. *Roadtrip Nation: A Guide to Discovering Your Path in Life*. New York: Ballantine Books.

Morgan, Adam. 1999. *Eating the Big Fish: How Challenger Brands Can Compete Against Brand Leaders*. New York: Wiley.

Petrini, Carlo, ed. 2003. *Slow Food: The Case for Taste*. New York: Columbia University Press.

Pirsig, Robert M. 1974. *Zen and the Art of Motorcycle Maintenance: An Inquiry into Values*. New York: Bantam Books.

Ries, Al, and Laura Ries. 2002. *The 22 Immutable Laws of Branding: How to Build a Product or Service into a World-Class Brand*. New York: HarperBusiness.

Schlosser, Eric. 2002. *Fast Food Nation: The Dark Side of the All-American Meal*. New York: HarperCollins.

Schumacher, E. F. 1973. *Small Is Beautiful: Economics as if People Mattered*. New York: HarperCollins.

Streb, Marla. 2003. *The Life Story of a Downhill Gravity Goddess*. New York: Plume.

Weber, Larry. 2001. *The Provocateur: How a New Generation of Leaders Are Building Communities, Not Just Companies*. New York: Crown Books.

ACKNOWLEDGMENTS

This is my first book. Since it tells the story not only of Clif Bar but also of my life, there are many people to thank. I've been fortunate to have great traveling companions.

Thanks to Susan Williams of Jossey-Bass for believing in this book and the story of Clif Bar. Thanks to many others at Jossey-Bass who were enthusiastic about *Raising the Bar*'s message, including President Debra Hunter, Rob Brandt, Byron Schneider, Paula Goldstein, Ralph Fowler, and Jeff Wyneken. Amy Rennert, my high-powered, incredibly bright and talented agent, guided me through the publishing process. Thanks to Mark Tauber, who was the first person in the publishing world to help me negotiate its unknown terrain and encourage me to write this book. Teresa Walsh "polished" this work with her astute editing. Leslie Henrichsen, my Head Sherpa (personal assistant) at Clif, not only greatly contributed to this book through fact checking, editing, and logistics but also stood by my side every day since I decided to walk away from the sale of Clif.

Jay Thomas, my white-road companion, continues to teach me how to be honest and to pursue life to its fullest. Thanks for all the great tours in the Alps and on rock, snow, and ice! I'm also fortunate to have traveled Europe's white roads with Paul McKenzie, Clem Donahue, Michael Kelley, Tom Bowman, Barry Schwartz, Darren Mar-Elia, Bill Morris, and Nick Zvegintzov. Thanks too to Jobst Brandt, the inventor of traveling light in the Alps. Many friends inspire me with their white-road journeys through life: Kelton (Tad) Cobb, Heidi Gehman, Deb Murray, George McKinley, Mark and Spider Cantley, Dave Willis, Jim and Lori Elliot, Nina Birnbaum, Greg Bagni, Cathy Tagudin, Wendy Diamond, the late Sally Peterson, Steve Reed, Julie Christinson Carlson, Bruce Hendricks, Sheila Ilsicin Hendricks, the late Greg Vette, Laurie Vette, John Tounger, Dave Estes and Kate Bevington, Steve and Sonia Chang, Casey Shaw, Pat Reedy, Herb Masters, Michael Moore, Garth Jaehnig, "Doc," Daniel Stebbins Park, Ron Kauk, Mike Cobb, Dan Kaufman, and all the Sierra Treks crew are just a few traveling companions. To the Mastrodicasa family in Florence; Paolo and Nene in Bassano del Grappa; and Guiseppe Bigolin and his family in Rossano Veneto—thanks for teaching me how to savor life the Italian way.

Many have guided me: coaches, teachers, entrepreneurs, mentors, bosses, even people who offered words of wisdom during brief encounters. I have learned from Lanny Vincent, David Batstone, Frank Mangiola, Richard Levin, Larry Jonutz, Jay Rizzetto, Yvon and Malinda Chouinard, the Baja boys, Harold Rothman, Bill Ross, Bill Roland, Dick Butterfield, Ben Cohen, Greg Steltenpohl, Ken Grossman, Jeremiah Pick, Mo Siegel,

Gil Pritchard, Al Springer, Bob Gamgort, Tom Ritchey, Jim Gentes, Rob Roskopp, Tracy Wong, Jim Collins, Patrick Lee, Michael Funk, Guru Dhan Klasna, Melodie Schneider, Lorraine Kaiser, the late Andrea Martin, Keith Kato, Doug Frank, Tyler Hamilton, Julia Butterfly Hill, Jeanne Rizzo, Sam Harrosh, Bill and Joan Keyser, Dennis Delatori, Lorenzo Petroni, and Jay Hammond.

I've received excellent legal counsel along the way. My attorney and confidant Bruce Lymburn has been at my side every step of the way since I decided to keep Clif Bar. I've also received valuable legal advice and assistance from Dick Lyons, Walter Turner, David Gaw, Lynn Perry, and David Goldman.

We were all saddened by the untimely death of Brian Maxwell, the founder of PowerBar. Brian made an enormous contribution to our industry by creating the energy bar category.

TO THE PEOPLE OF CLIF BAR, PAST AND PRESENT: Without you the company and this story would not exist. I wish I could mention each of you by name, but Lois said the book would be too long! Thank you for believing in the vision and for knowing that we could get through difficult times. Your enthusiasm, spirit, creativity, hard work, and passion for life inspire me.

Doug Gilmour trusted in my vision from the early days to the present: thanks for your never-ending incredible contribution to the Gary Bar . . . I mean Clif Bar journey, and to this book. Thanks to Sheryl O'Loughlin, Stan Tanka, and David Jericoff, for being such trusted stewards of the company and for your

RAISING THE BAR

THE STORY OF CLIF BAR, INC.

contributions to *Raising the Bar*. Paul McKenzie, Thao Pham, Cassie Cyphers, Janet Minix wrote sidebars for us and made sure we got our facts right. Leif Eric Arneson rates special thanks for his creative designs for the book proposal, jacket cover, images, and layout for *Raising the Bar*. I will forever thank Elysa Hammond for introducing me to Kit and for guiding Clif on our journey to sustainability. Thanks for your passion and friendship.

To my dear friend Lois (a.k.a. Zoe, Zo, Loie, Purchase, Sybil—don't ask): Who would have thought that twenty-five years after we first met, while guiding junior high kids together high in the Sierra with Sierra Treks, that we would actually write a book together? Our friendship has grown ever since and it made perfect sense that we would write *Raising the Bar* together. Lois knows me, and the story of Clif Bar, very well; it seemed like a perfect match. Her brilliance and creativity added to this book—thanks for keeping my voice. Thanks for your passion and incredible devotion over the last many months to make this story come alive.

My YaYa (grandmother) left us in 1989, four years after I named the original company after her—Kali's. I still miss her. My brother Randy has taught me much about business, creativity, engineering, cooking, and life. Thanks bro, for all you contribute to Clif Bar on a daily basis and for helping me with this book. My brother David has taught me much about life through his determination and never-give-up attitude. I'm amazed at his ability to make art express who he is. My parents, Cliff and Mary Erickson, taught me how to be free and independent, and never held me back from exploring the world and my place in it. Mom—thanks for teaching me how to bake, play the piano, and appreciate art. Dad—thanks for introducing me to the outdoors, and especially to the Sierra Nevada range of California. Your commitment to each other has been a model for me in my relationships to the world, my friends, my business, and especially to my family and life partner.

Kit and I are blessed with extended families who never waver in their support. I'm grateful. My beloved children, Kate, Clayton, and Lydia, humble me and teach me what life is about daily. Kit continues to amaze me with her patience, bravery, and kindness in all that she is and does. I'm thankful every day for her commitment to me and to our wonderful company.

Lois thanks the great people at Clif Bar who were patient, kind, and helpful as she pestered them while working on this book. Doug Gilmour, Paul McKenzie, Sheryl O'Loughlin, David Jericoff, Stan Tanka, Randy Erickson, Thao Pham, Cassie Cyphers, Janet Minix, and Clif attorney Bruce Lymburn generously gave their time to read portions of the manuscript, talk with me, and make sure I got it right. Leif Eric Arneson's creativity is evident through his design of the proposal, jacket cover, chapter, and images in *Raising the Bar*. A big thanks to Leslie Henrichsen for being my own personal "Pace Team." I first met Elysa Hammond while roaming the Sierra Nevada mountain range, and it's been a gift to work with her again after all these years. Mark Tauber graciously read proposal drafts, answered e-mail, and offered his considerable wisdom of the publishing world. Thanks to Amy Rennert, agent extraordinaire, for enthusiasm

RAISING THE BAR

THE STORY OF CLIF BAR, INC.

and knowledge. The Jossey-Bass crowd provided consistent support and assistance. Thanks to Rob Brandt, Byron Schneider, Jeff Wyneken, and especially to Susan Williams: your enthusiasm for this project motivated us.

The University of San Francisco (USF) provides me with great colleagues and a supportive work environment. Thanks especially to Jennifer Turpin, a constant friend, support, and "partner in crime" over the years. Mike Duffy and David Batstone are amazing colleagues: thanks for your friendship, laughter, and commitment to making the world a better place. Tracy Seeley and Vijaya Nagarajan provided oases of warmth and sanity when I emerged from my computer cave. Thanks to Shelley Tito who took care of the Religion and Immigration (TRIP) details while I worked on *Raising the Bar*. The immigration project researchers Kevin Chun, Hien Duc Do, Jay Gonzalez, Susan Zaraysky, Luis Enrique Bazan, Rosalina Mira, Lorrie Ranck, honorary member Jerry Berndt, and all the "trippers" continually inspire me with their dedication, compassion, and intelligence.

Teresa Walsh helped craft this book; she is without a doubt one of the world's most gifted and creative editors (and people). A big thanks T!

Writing this book with Gary made me nostalgic for my Sierra Treks friends and for months roaming the high Sierra together; you remain the greatest, most fun and passionate crowd I know. *Las Mujeres,* Maria Jose Perry, Brianna Leavitt, and Teresa Walsh gave me "sister" support. The friendship of my San Francisco family sustained me: thanks Bob, Clark, Brad, Benjamin,

Rusty, Dave, Wendy, Jade, Zach, Jesse, and Caelin. My sister Ruth Ann called me literally every day to make sure I didn't become a complete hermit—thanks sis! And, thanks to the rest of my great family who shared their enthusiasm for *Raising the Bar*. Doctor Ernest and Nelia Lorentzen (mom and dad) and brothers Peter, Paul, Mark, and their fantastic families continually brighten my life.

This book wouldn't have been possible without Cliff and Mary Erickson—thanks for starting it all! During the writing of this book, Kit, Gary, Lydia, Clayton, and Kate warmly invited me into their home. Thanks for being such a fantastic second family.

Gerardo Marin, as always, grounded me with his calm, love, and support (and great cooking!).

Finally, thanks to Gary for being a great friend. Thanks for the great climbs, backpacking epics, winter camping and skiing adventures, intense conversations, and laughter. It was fun, easy, intense, and deeply rewarding to work on *Raising the Bar* together. Thanks for bringing your vision into the world!

INDEX

RAISING THE BAR

THE STORY OF CLIF BAR, INC.

Raising the Bar Facts (Post Publication)

Activity	Difference
Companies Saved	1 (in millions)
Salsa Dance classes taken	500,000
Alpine Bike Tours taken	5K
Pounds&Inches lost	67,000#, 976M"
Partners Bought Out	5x1,000C
Mojo Regained	500,000
New Companies started	500K
Organic Farms saved	400 (in thousands)
Gross National Morale Increase	250%
Magic Moments	Countless

INGREDIENTS

Refinance debt, free cashflow (with added working capital management), tax planning, lower cost of goods, regular budget reviews (with re-alignment of spend to sales), low inventory levels, investing in training and education, good forecasting, Annual Incentive Plan, Epiphany Ride, Martini & Weenie Party, camping trip, ski trip, Pac Bell Park (Sec 128, Row 18, Seats 5,6,7,8), Iron Chef competition, gym, wellness program, concierge services, fabulous holiday party, sabbatical leave, 9/80 workweek, future childcare, bagel, donuts, snack central, goldfish, orange slices, red vines, sour punch twists. Santa Clara Co. Diabetes Society, The Breast Cancer Peak Hike, Habitat for Humanity, Sports for Kids, Ma & Pa Green, LunaFest, Luna Chix, Ambassodors, consumer service, public relations, website, dedications, The Breast Cancer Fund, athletic sponsorships, USPS Cycling Team, Beyond the Podium, Clif Cross Team, seasonal flavors, new flavors, the introduction of MOJO, events (Escape from Alcatraz, Sea Otter, Marine Corps. Marathon, Chicago Marathon, Tuscon Marathon...etc.), direct mail, merchandisers, strategic promotions, sales, collateral, free samples, awesome sales/marketing plan quality assurance program, in-house R&D, field reps, regional sales. 2nd Start Adult Literacy, Friends of Five Creeks, meals on Wheels, Adopt-A-Trail, PAWS, AIDS Walk, Cinderella ride, Circle of Life, Disabled Sports USA, Alameda Co. Food Bank, Peralta Elementary School, East Bay Fire Fighters, East Bay Pride, Georgetown High School,Brower Youth, Rose Day, Berkeley Booster, Markie Foundation, Leukemia & Lymphoma Society, Mentoring, Read Aloud Day. **STAY TUNED...**

Gary Erickson is the founder and owner of Clif Bar Inc., a company that made the Inc. 500—*Inc.* magazine's list of the fastest-growing privately held companies four years running. Clif Bar Inc. remains one of the nation's fastest-growing private companies. He has been featured in *People* magazine, *Inc.* magazine, *Health, Fortune Small Business,* the *San Francisco Chronicle, Reader's Digest,* and in numerous other publications. Erickson is a frequent speaker in a wide variety of venues and has won numerous awards. He brings his background as a competitive cyclist, jazz musician, world traveler, gourmet cook, mountain climber, wilderness guide, and father to *Raising the Bar.* Gary Erickson lives in northern California with his wife, children, horses, dogs, and bikes.

Lois Ann Lorentzen is professor of social ethics at the University of San Francisco. She serves on the board of the Leo T. McCarthy Center for Public Service and the Common Good, the Center for Latino Studies in the Americas, and the Religion and Immigration Project. She has seven books to her credit, contributes frequently to magazines and journals, and has won numerous academic awards.

Erickson and Lorentzen first met while working for Sierra Treks, a wilderness organization. Over the course of their twenty-five-year friendship they have climbed mountains together, bicycled, skied, winter-camped, and talked about the dreams and values that define Clif Bar Inc. and *Raising the Bar*.

RAISING
THE
BAR

THE STORY OF CLIF BAR, INC.